David
Beckham
My Son

David Beckham My Son

Ted Beckham
with Tim Allan

PAN BOOKS

First published 2005 by Boxtree

First published in paperback 2006 by Pan Books

This edition published 2007 by Pan Books
an imprint of Pan Macmillan Ltd
Pan Macmillan, 20 New Wharf Road, London N1 9RR
Basingstoke and Oxford
Associated companies throughout the world
www.panmacmillan.com

ISBN 978-0-330-45302-8

1 3 5 7 9 8 6 4 2

A CIP catalogue record for this book is available from
the British Library.

Designed and typeset by Perfect Bound Ltd
Printed by Mackays of Chatham plc, Chatham, Kent

Visit **www.panmacmillan.com** to read more about all our books and to buy
them. You will also find features, author interviews and news of any author
events, and you can sign up for e-newsletters so that you're always first to hear
about our new releases.

CONTENTS

PROLOGUE:
26 MAY 1999

My nerves were jangling as I took my seat in the Nou Camp Stadium for the biggest game of my son's life – Manchester United v Bayern Munich in the 1999 European Cup Final.

This was it – the pinnacle of my son's career and of my footballing dream.

My boy, David Beckham, was playing for my team, Manchester United, in the biggest game ever played by a British club. He was a vital member of a team which had already stunned English football by winning both the Premiership and the FA Cup. Now they stood on the brink of an unprecedented treble.

The final was being held in one of the world's great sporting arenas – Barcelona's Nou Camp. The stands seem to rise almost vertically above the ground to create a cauldron of noise, colour and atmosphere. On that hot, sunny evening, those stands were packed with 90,000 screaming, passionate fans.

The gnawing tension had been building inside me for a week, just as it had for David. As the players started their pre-match warm-ups, I could hardly bear to sit in my seat. The nerves and the pressure had really got to me – seconds turned to minutes and minutes to hours. My mouth had gone dry and the clamour all around me seemed strangely distant, as though I were looking through the wrong end of a telescope.

My wife, Sandra, was beside me and there were familiar faces all around but all I could concentrate on was my son. His performance was the most important thing to me – I knew if he played well, then United had a fantastic chance of claiming the ultimate prize in club football.

David caught my eye and gave a little wave, as he always did before every game. Sandra and I smiled back, trying to look both calm and determined.

The game kicked off but the tension had got to the United players. Passes were misplaced, nothing flowed and neither team really got into its stride. Yet that only made my nerves worse – I knew one little mistake might decide the outcome.

Even though I'd watched David play countless hundreds of games, I struggled to put my finger on what was wrong with him or the team. Bayern were typically well-organized and gave nothing away at the back, while United, without suspended midfielders Roy Keane and Paul Scholes, looked disjointed and out of sorts.

But nothing prepared us for the opening goal – scored by the Germans after just six minutes. United's Ronny Johnsen conceded a free-kick just outside the penalty area and Mario Basler slammed the ball home.

From that moment on, the Germans battered us. They hit the bar and Peter Schmeichel in the United goal made several outstanding saves.

The game and the chance of making history seemed to be slipping away. At half-time, the United fans looked tense and nervous, unable to understand how the flowing football which had dominated the English season had disappeared. Somehow, the glamour of the occasion had been replaced by pure tension which no-one in a United shirt was enjoying.

I exchanged a few brief words with Sandra and the people around me. I've no idea what I said or what they said to me. My mind was in a jumble and my nerves had got worse and worse but, at only 1–0 down, we still had a chance.

The second half started much like the first, with the Germans on top and threatening to run away with the game. But with 20 minutes to go they had a decision to make – should they try and hold what they had or keep going for another goal?

They chose the first option and took off inspirational midfielder Lotthar Matthaus and striker Alexander Zickler in an attempt to hold on for a 1–0 win. United threw everything forward, replacing winger Jesper Blomqvist and centre-forward Andy Cole with strikers Teddy Sheringham and Ole Gunnar Solskjaer.

With five minutes to go, it looked like the Germans had got it right. The United players were driving themselves towards the Bayern goal but nothing seemed to be working. Then a high ball came out of the United defence towards David, who was standing in the centre circle. I watched as he headed it forward and, with United pouring forward, Bayern were forced to concede a corner-kick.

David sprinted over to take it. This was the moment we had been preparing for all his life, all those countless hours spent practising corner-kick after corner-kick on muddy, windswept pitches in east London. All that practice was about to pay off in the most spectacular fashion.

He took his familiar run-up, arching his body sideways, his left arm outstretched, as his right boot connected with the ball to send over a devastatingly accurate centre. The United keeper Schmeichel had come up into the German penalty area in a last desperate attempt to score. The Bayern defenders looked utterly confused as Dwight Yorke headed the ball backwards for Ryan Giggs to fire goalwards. As the ball rebounded, Teddy Sheringham reacted first to stab home a sensational equalizer.

'Yeeeeessssssssss!' I roared as the whole United end leapt skywards and the entire stadium seemed to turn red and white. I was dancing around like a lunatic and punching the air in jubilation.

With just four minutes left to play, it was 1–1. Now United had the momentum and the Germans looked stunned. They had been just seconds away from getting their hands on the European Cup – suddenly they were staring at extra time. Or so they thought.

Just three minutes later and with the German fans whistling madly for the ref to blow for full-time, United won another corner. It was on the same side as the goal had come from, right in front of the main block of United support.

The noise was deafening as David ran over to take it again. He stood with his hands on his hips, eyeing up the penalty area and imagining the ball swinging into the danger area. With one deep breath, he ran forwards, arching his body again, to get the maximum amount of power and curve on the ball. I watched open-mouthed as the ball curled into the penalty area and the players jostled for the final touch.

This time, Sheringham got his head to the ball first. We watched as it bounced over the German defenders towards the far post, where the little Norwegian Solskjaer was waiting. We rose to our feet and our arms started to reach skywards as Solskjaer reacted instantly to hook the ball into the net and score the winning goal.

Up we went again, totally overcome with joy. The huge out-pouring of pent-up emotion swept across the stadium as Solskjaer was enveloped by his delirious team-mates. Unbelievably, incredibly, astonishingly, United were 2–1 ahead with just seconds to go. The European Cup – and a place in footballing immortality – was ours.

That final minute was one of the happiest of my life. The Germans were shot to pieces – they could barely comprehend what had happened and were never going to come back. In the space of just 240 seconds, United had gone from losers to treble winners and my son had been at the centre of it all.

As the final whistle went, I cheered deliriously, hugging anyone who came near me. The tears welled in my eyes as I thought back to how my son's incredible journey to the pinnacle of world football had begun. And then they flowed uncontrollably down my cheeks, as the pride in both my team and my son overwhelmed me.

FROM WHIPPS CROSS TO WADHAM LODGE
1975-1982

'Dad – one day I'm going to play for Manchester United.'

A million fathers must have heard those words and never expected them to come true. Well, they did for me.

The first match I ever took David to was Tottenham v Manchester United on 6 September 1980. A 0–0 draw but still enough to confirm my son's love affair with the club I'd supported all my life.

He was five at the time, still too young to really understand football, but old enough to know he loved everything about the game.

We set off from our home in Chingford around lunchtime. David was wearing his United tracksuit and was thrilled to be seeing his team in action. I drove down to White Hart Lane in my old Escort van and got there good and early to miss all the crowds. We parked near the ground and made our way through the tatty backstreets to the stadium, his tiny hand gripping mine tightly.

It was still too early for most fans. There were just a few supporters wearing their colours but none of the expectant buzz you get just before kick-off. I carried David through the turnstiles and we took our seats, high above the pitch. It must have looked enormous to the tiny, fair-haired boy sat beside me.

I looked around the almost empty stands, thrilled to be taking my son to his first game. The lack of atmosphere didn't spoil it for David, though. Just to be going to a game was making his dream come true.

As kick-off approached he got more and more excited. We had to make a couple of trips to the toilet – always a sure sign of nerves in him, both then and now.

The teams appeared on the pitch and I picked him up to get a better view. He cheered and cheered as United ran on; occasionally glancing up at me to make sure I was watching him. I'd never seen him more thrilled.

The game passed him in a blur and I can't pretend he took it all in. I had a good supply of chocolate buttons in my pocket and kept feeding them to him when his interest wandered. We left just before the end to miss the crowds but it was still the happiest day of his life. He'd seen the mighty Reds in action and even though there'd been no goals, he had been captivated by the whole atmosphere of the game.

I felt just as happy as him. To see his face light up had been worth the price of the tickets alone. What made him happy made me happy. It was true then and it's still true today.

As I carried him down the terrace steps, he looked at me and said, 'Dad, one day I'm going to play for Manchester United.'

'I'll come and watch you, even if you're playing for Barnet,' I laughed.

Of course, I didn't know then his incredible journey to the top of world football would take me to far more exotic places than that.

That journey started when I married Sandra in the autumn of 1969. It hadn't exactly been a whirlwind romance – we'd been courting for a good few years before I finally plucked up the courage to ask her to be my wife.

Our first child, Lynne, arrived three years later, although she came into the world without her father there. I'd been sent home by the nurses, who assured me nothing was going to happen for ages. Of course, she was born while I was fast asleep at home.

That made me even more determined to be there for the birth of our second child on 2 May 1975 in Whipps Cross Hospital, East London. David was born at 6.17am and weighed 7lb 6oz.

'Congratulations, Dad – it's a boy,' said the midwife as she cleaned him up and put him in my arms.

I defy any dad in the world not to have a tear in his eye when he hears those words. I was no different, and it's impossible to describe the overwhelming feeling of love I had when I looked down and saw my son lying in my arms.

I was thrilled to have a boy. I had always been passionate about football and had only given up playing when I'd got married. My career had never really amounted to much – trials with Leyton Orient and a few seasons of senior amateur football with Leyton Wingate – but as I looked down at our new baby, I dreamed of what might be.

We decided on his names almost there and then. Both Sandra and I liked the name David for two reasons: first, it's a strong name and secondly, it's my proper Christian name, even though I've been known as Ted or Teddy all my life.

Edward is my middle name but both my father and grandfather were called Ted and they were determined to carry on the family tradition. So no matter how much my mum may have wanted me to be David, they made sure I was another Ted.

David's middle names are Robert, after Bobby Charlton, the greatest Manchester United player of his day and a real hero of mine; and Joseph, after Sandra's dad, a passionate Tottenham fan and a big influence on David's early life.

Like most dads, I was determined to give my children a better start in life than I'd had. My parents, Doris and Ted, had worked hard to give the best they could to me and my younger brother, John, but life was a struggle.

The fee or this
certificate is 3s. 0d. (25p)

CAUTION—Any person who (1) falsifies any
of the particulars on this certificate, or (2) uses
a falsified certificate as true knowing it to be
false, is liable to prosecution.

CERTIFIED COPY OF AN ENTRY
Pursuant to the Births and Deaths Registration Act 1953

NHS Number		**BIRTH**		Entry No.

Registration district	WALTHAM FOREST		Administrative area	
Sub-district	WALTHAM FOREST	LONDON BOROUGH OF WALTHAM FOREST		

CHILD

1. Date and place of birth — *Second May 1975, Whipps Cross Hospital, Leytonstone*

2. Name and surname — *David Robert Joseph BECKHAM* | 3. Sex — *Male*

FATHER

4. Name and surname — *David Edward Alan BECKHAM*

5. Place of birth — *Edmonton, Enfield*

6. Occupation — *Maintenance Gas Fitter*

MOTHER

7. Name and surname — *Sandra Georgina BECKHAM*

8. Place of birth — *Islington*

9. (a) Maiden surname — *WEST* | (b) Surname at marriage if different from maiden surname — —

10. Usual address (if different from place of child's birth) — *155 Norman Road, E.11.*

INFORMANT

11. Name and surname (if not the mother or father) — — | 12. Qualification — *Mother*

13. Usual address (if different from that in 10 above)

14. I certify that the particulars entered above are true to the best of my knowledge and belief

.... *S. G. Beckham* .... of Signature of informant

15. Date of registration — *Eleventh June 1975* | 16. Signature of registrar — *D. Workman, Registrar*

17. Name given after registration, and surname

Certified to be a true copy of an entry in a register in my custody.

.... *D. Workman* .... Registrar .... *11/6/75* .... Date

B. Cert.
R.B.D.

David's birth certificate.

I was born in Forest Gate, London, but we moved to Sheerness in Kent when I was three or four. My dad was a sweetmaker by trade and he'd got a job on the coast making rock and candies for holidaymakers. We lived in a small, terraced house not far from the seafront and money was always tight.

I remember my dad watching me play football, but I always got the impression he wasn't all that bothered about the game. He had a casual interest in how Arsenal had got on but he was never passionate about it. I was determined that wouldn't happen with David. I wanted to pass on my passion for the game to him and make sure I was always there for him.

I've supported United for as long as I can remember. I used to sit with my dad on Saturday afternoons listening to the football results and I just loved the sound of 'Manchester United'. To me, even the name seemed glamorous and exciting.

I was about ten years old when the Munich Air Disaster happened in February 1958. My dad told me about it when he came home from work and it was all over the radio and the papers.

I couldn't believe it. I was devastated but that awful feeling only confirmed my support. I was hooked on United then, I still am now and I always will be.

We moved back to London when I was about twelve, first to Lewisham and then to Leytonstone. Dad's work brought us back and Mum was also working full-time in a factory making lead seals, as well as bringing up me and John, who is seven years my junior.

My mum passed away when she was only 41 and I was just 23. She died of stomach and chest cancer and it was very hard to watch her go downhill. She had been a strikingly beautiful woman, tall with lovely dark hair, but we could do nothing as she just wasted away. It affected us all very badly, especially John, and forced us to become very self-sufficient and not take anything for granted.

Some years later my dad remarried and moved away. At first, I used to see him every week, then every month and by the time he died seven or eight years ago it was really only at Christmas. It was a shame my kids never got to know my parents really well but I'm sure many families have similar stories to tell.

Sandra took on most of the work of looking after the children when they were young – I only ever changed one nappy in my life, on Lynne, and that was a complete disaster. Sandra made sure they always had a good routine – the three Bs: bath, bottle and bed – and they were usually all tucked up by 7.30pm and listening, as they drifted off to sleep, to one of our 30-odd collection of pre-recorded fairytale cassettes. She really did a fantastic job when they were young and I'm sure that stood them in good stead as they were growing up.

We moved around a lot in those early days. We started in a small flat in Walthamstow, then went to the sixth floor of a tower block in Chingford, then to a three-bedroom house in Leytonstone, which is where we were living when David arrived. But within three years we'd moved back to Chingford, first to Rowden Park Gardens and then to Hampton Road, which is where I still live today.

There's nothing special about the road, which is just a couple of hundred yards north of the North Circular, or the house, a three-bedroom terrace. The road is just about wide enough for two cars to pass and most of the front gardens have been concreted over for parking. The best thing about the house as far as David was concerned was the 140ft long garden – perfect for a kickabout with Dad – and the fact that there was a big park within 100 yards of the front door.

Money was very tight in those days and I was working all the time to try and make ends meet. I'd left school at 15 without a qualification to my name and had done a variety of jobs – I was a waiter at Browns Hotel, then I helped out in a wood shop and after that I worked alongside my mum in the factory.

My dream at school had been to play professional football but when I went for careers advice the guy just said to me, 'Can you imagine how many people want to become footballers? You've got no chance.'

By the time David arrived, I was working for a firm called Benham's, doing heating and ventilation installations on large buildings. I'd started out at a small building firm, doing repointing and roofing work, but I walked out when the boss wouldn't give me an afternoon off to celebrate my engagement. That was typical of me back then, and it's still true now. Once I've made up my mind to do something, I do it and no one can talk me out of it.

I was on the dole for a few months before a family friend, Jack Owen, got me the job at Benham's. The first site I ever worked on was in Lombard Street, where we were building a bank and I was doing 70 or 80 hours a week. I often worked nights and did loads of overtime to earn extra money but, of course, it meant I missed out on seeing a lot of the children when they were small. That is probably my one major regret.

About every three months or so, I used to go to Cambridge for a week because we had the contract to service and repair the university kitchens. I lived in digs with a couple of mates and while we had a good laugh up there, I know it was hard for Sandra trying to run the house and bring up the children.

Then, when David was about six, I accepted a contract to work in Saudi Arabia for three months. I'd discussed it with Sandra and we'd decided we had to take the chance to earn some decent money, even if it meant being away for a long time.

I'd committed to it more than a year before the job began but by the time it came round I was having second thoughts because Sandra was pregnant.

But there was no way out and we needed the money, so off I went. We were working on a Royal Saudi Air Force base in Tarbuk, near the Jordanian border. Believe it or not, I played more football out there than I would have done at home. We played six-a-side games most evenings and then organized full-scale 11-a-side games against teams of Germans, French and the Arabs.

Unfortunately, Sandra had a miscarriage while I was in Saudi. I got a phone call from her mum telling me what had happened. I was all for coming home straight away but she assured me Sandra was OK and persuaded me to see out the contract. After I got that news, I couldn't wait to get home.

It was only when I came home that I learned the truth – that Sandra had suffered problems after the miscarriage and had been forced to spend several days in hospital. Her parents had stayed at our house to look after Lynne and David.

I arrived home in the November and as we flew in over London I could see the frost and snow on the ground. The bitter cold hit me as I walked off the plane, wearing just a shirt and a cardigan, which was all I'd needed for three months. I sat on the train back to Walthamstow freezing my wotsits off, with people staring at me as though I were mad. They were all there in their hats, coats and scarves and I had nothing warm to put on.

Sandra and the two children met me at the station. As I got off the train and walked up the platform, Lynne and David started running towards me. I could see they were both crying and I welled up as well. It was fantastic to see them after so long away. They threw their arms around me and I gave Lynne a great big cuddle and swept David up to give him a hug. Then Lynne held my hand as I carried David in the other arm up to where Sandra was. It was a very emotional time and all the more memorable for that.

The kids were thrilled to see me and neither of them left my side. We got home and I opened up the suitcase and dished out all the presents. In fact, I'd spent so much on presents that we didn't do all that well out of it in the end.

I threw myself back into the family and work and it wasn't long before David's younger sister Joanne came along.

On the day she was born, in 1982, I got back from the hospital and said to Lynne and David, 'Mum's had a baby.'

'What's she had?' said David.

'A little girl—'

'I DON'T WANT A GIRL, I WANT A BOY.'

He started crying, he was so disappointed. He'd set his heart on a brother – someone else to play football with. But we took him up to the hospital and as soon as he saw her, his mood changed. They've been close ever since and Joanne was always happy to kick a ball in the back garden with him, so he got the best of both worlds.

David and Joanne are seven years apart but she has always looked up to him and he's always looked out for her. That probably dates from the time when Joanne was about 18 months old and she pulled David's hair. She really hurt him and he cried like anything. We told her it was naughty but to teach her a lesson I pulled her hair back.

Well, that was it. She cried and cried and then started holding her breath. She just wouldn't breathe and then, to our horror, she passed out. David was terrified, blaming himself for what had happened. We didn't know what to do. First, we tried to give her mouth-to-mouth resuscitation. When that didn't work, Sandra and I got her in my van and took her to the doctor's. He wasn't in, so we headed off to the hospital.

It was a nightmare journey, the traffic was bad and all the lights were against us and still Joanne wasn't breathing. She'd turned blue and we were really panicking. Then, all of a sudden, she just woke up and said: 'What's going on? Where are we going?' Apparently, kids can do that if they get themselves really worked up.

We were all so relieved that she was all right, especially David because he had been so worried. When we got home he was all over her, making sure she was OK. After that, Joanne got away

21

with everything. She could hit him, pull his hair, kick him and he wouldn't react for fear of seeing her pass out again.

When she was older, Joanne was the perfect goalkeeper for David's football games in the back garden. She's always loved being with her big brother and, when David's career started to progress, we always took her with us to games.

Between them, they wrecked our garden. There wasn't a flower left alive. I used to have a go at both of them about it, but I was never too serious. I was a lot more interested in football than gardening.

David often used to torment his sisters but somehow he would get away with it. He and Lynne used to argue quite a lot and they never really saw eye to eye while they were growing up. They'd argue about little things the whole time, like whose turn it was in the bathroom. Sandra would run a bath and David would push in front of Lynne to get in it first. There'd be a huge screaming match but David would usually stay in the bath and there wasn't much Lynne could do about it.

I'm sure that goes on in all families and I'm just as sure our children had a very happy upbringing.

Some of the happiest times we had as a family were at Christmas, when Sandra's mum and dad would come over and we'd push the boat out for the kids.

On Christmas morning, we would make the three children wait at the top of the stairs while I went down to check if Father Christmas had been. In reality, I was setting up the cinecamera to capture the excitement on their faces as they came through the door and saw their bulging stockings around the fireplace.

It became a Christmas tradition that I would buy David a new Manchester United kit and Sandra's dad would buy him a new Tottenham strip. We'd get him to put them on and there was always plenty of banter about who he would end up playing for. He ended up with loads of football kits – Barcelona, AC Milan, even Manchester City, which I bought through gritted teeth. I've still got all the old kits he used to wear – the whole lot, shirts, shorts and everything.

I remember one Christmas he was desperate to have a new bike. Of course, Sandra took him to the shop and he picked out the most expensive one on the rack. She showed him a couple of the cheaper ones, but he'd set his heart on the top-of-the-range model.

Sandra warned him we might not be able to afford it. Of course, we found the money from somewhere and bought him the bike.

I have to say it was worth every penny to see his face on that Christmas morning. He was so thrilled – and so grateful. He knew we'd had to make a few sacrifices to pay for it and that made it all the more special for him.

He taught himself to ride that bike. He just jumped on and off he went. I suppose he was about six or seven. I went over to the park one day and there he was, riding around on a great big grown-up bike. I had no idea who it belonged to but he didn't have a care in the world and certainly no fear. That was the great thing about him, even at that age, he had so much confidence in his own ability. He's always had great balance and I suppose that made riding a bike that much easier.

We always made sure we celebrated the children's birthdays properly, even though they received the biggest presents at Christmas. We usually organized a meal out for the five of us on their birthdays, often at a local pub called the Green Man. It was just a Beefeater-style restaurant but the staff knew us and always made it special for the children.

David was good at every sport he tried – and still is. He's a strong swimmer and brilliant at all ball sports – pool, snooker, table tennis, golf. I know he sounds too good to be true, but that's the way he was.

Obviously, there were times when I had to tell him off. He was a bit cheeky as a youngster and I had to warn him about that a few times but I honestly cannot remember a single major incident. It was very low-level stuff and he always knew where to draw the line. I think he got away with things a bit more with his mum but he knew when I said something I meant it. I was pretty strict with all of the children but I think it was good for them to know where the boundaries were.

If he wasn't kicking a ball as a kid, he would be playing with his toy cars and Lego. He had boxes and boxes of cars and used to spend hours playing with them. He liked to line them all up and have races, and then he would use the Lego to build bridges, ramps and circuits for them.

We bought him Scalextric one Christmas and he really loved that. He was pretty good at it but a bit like he is now as a driver – erratic! Some days he'd take it nice and easy and control the cars really well, other days he'd go mad and they would fly off at almost every corner. Mind you, when he got the hang of it, he used to beat me hands down.

I also did my best to get him into Airfix model aeroplane kits, which I myself had loved as a child. We spent hours putting them together when he was small and then I painted them all and hung them on his bedroom ceiling. We made it look like they were having dogfights, with flames on the German ones and cotton wool trailing off them to make it look like smoke was coming out of their engines. I broke a couple of them to make it look like they'd been hit in battle and were falling out of the sky. He had Spitfires, Hurricanes, Messerschmitts, Stukas and Lancaster bombers up there – it looked really good. David loved it at night, because he would lie in his bed with a torch shining up at them, bringing the whole scene to life.

When Joanne arrived, David had to move into the small box room so she and Lynne could share. It was about 8ft by 6ft – just big enough for a bed, a wardrobe and loads of football posters. His great heroes were Bryan Robson and Mark Hughes and the walls were covered in their pictures. Then we bought him a United bedspread and pillow case, plus United curtains, so his room turned into an Old Trafford shrine.

He wasn't into books – unless they were about football. He loved *Shoot* magazine and the football annuals he always got for Christmas and his birthday. He also loved the Panini sticker albums and always had a pocketful of the stickers to swap with his mates at school. They used to cost me a fortune because he always had to have the whole lot.

The one surprising thing about David was how neat and tidy he was – not something you can say of many boys. He loved looking smart and all his clothes had to match – if you suggested he put blue trousers with a red shirt, he would go mad. In fact, he was so neat that he even used to fold up his dirty laundry.

I remember when we threw a party for Sandra's dad on his 60th birthday and David looked superb. He was only seven or so, but he insisted on wearing a shirt, jumper and trousers with razor-sharp creases.

His room was always immaculate as well – unlike his two sisters. He hated having things out of place. He made his bed every morning and liked to have everything in order and shipshape. The only thing we ever told him off about was his clothes, because if he tried on some outfit in the morning and didn't like it, he'd just leave it on the bed and get another one out.

He had a dummy until he was six, when Sandra decided he had to give it up. She told him it was time for our pet rabbit to have it – a ruse, of course. She was expecting a big fuss but the next day, David dropped the dummy into the hutch and that was the end of it. He let go of it without any problems. He also had a light blue teddy bear – Manchester City blue, I'm ashamed to admit – which he always took to bed with him.

He didn't care much about his hair in those days. He pretty much kept the same style and we used to take him to a barber's in Chingford called Nice One, John. I think it used to cost me a couple of quid but I know he pays a bit more than that now.

One highlight of the year was our trip to the Royal Tournament at Olympia. I'd once had vague ambitions to follow my grandfather into the navy, so it was great to see all the service boys in action. David really loved it too.

One year we watched the soldiers leap off a balcony about 90ft off the ground and come down a sloping rope to the ground, hanging on to some sort of rolling pulley. At the end they asked if any kids wanted to do it and David just leapt up and said: 'I want to do that!' I was a bit nervous about letting him but he insisted. When he got to the balcony, he just hung on to the straps and leapt off. They grabbed him as he came to the end and he was beaming from ear to ear. No fear at all – he loved it.

He was just the same at theme parks, like Thorpe Park and Chessington Zoo. We used to take him but he would insist on going on all the big rides by himself. His mum and I were too scared and his sisters didn't want to know, but he loved the thrill of those rollercoasters.

David's first school, Chase Lane Primary, was just around the corner from home. It was only a two-minute walk but he took a ball with him every single day. He was great at getting up in the mornings but he wouldn't leave the house without a ball, so he'd sometimes make himself late by looking for one.

He was very happy at primary school and the teachers all loved him. He was never a bighead and he never wanted to show off. He was very respectful and never rude. We'd drummed it into all our children that being polite and remembering to say please and thank you can take you a long way. I can honestly say I can't remember him ever being in serious trouble at school. I know that sounds as though David was too good to be true, but that was the way it was.

You always knew when David was coming home because you'd

hear the ball being kicked long before you saw him. He'd play football on the way to school, in every break, at every lunchtime and on the way home from school.

Then, as soon as he got home, he'd get changed, grab a sandwich and then head over to the park for still more football. He'd come back hours later, starving hungry and wanting his mum to cook tea. As often as not, he would be over there with some of his big mates – kids like Nicky Lockwood and the Treglowen brothers, Matthew and Simon, who all lived very close to us.

They used to run through the alleyway opposite our house, duck under or through the hedge and be in the park. There wasn't much to Chase Lane Park back then – just a big grass area, about the size of three football pitches and a kids' playground with a paddling pool. There were no goalposts or pitch markings – the lads just used to throw down their jumpers and make believe it was Wembley.

Nicky was one of his biggest mates back then, as was a lad called John Brown. Strangely enough, John wasn't a passionate footballer, so he would often end up playing Lego or Gameboy with David. The two of them went through primary and secondary school together, so they knew each other inside out.

Another great friend of David's in those early days was Alan Smith, who was a few years older but lived next door to us. Alan wasn't really into football and didn't go over the park much but he and David always got on well together and Alan used to come into our house quite a lot just to hang out or play on the Gameboys.

From as early as I can remember, David put football above everything else. He was absolutely passionate about it.

He had tried to kick things almost from the moment he could walk. We started him off with rolled-up socks in the front room, which he would kick as hard as he could. His legs didn't really support him properly so he fell over all the time but he really loved it.

27

Then we bought him a small, plastic football which we let him use in the house. I was desperate to see him kicking a football, although I don't think his mum was too pleased! There's even a video of him when he was about 18 months old, sliding up and down the hall in his little Manchester United kit and a tiny pair of football boots.

He loved to watch football almost as much as he loved playing it. We always made a point of going to watch United if they were in London, especially at West Ham, Spurs and Arsenal because they were the easiest grounds for us to get to. Obviously, I was pushing him in one direction – I really wanted him to become as big a United fan as I was and I'm happy to say I succeeded.

David could always kick a ball and right from the start I made sure he practised. I'd just tell him to kick it as hard as he could. Even then, he could really whack a ball and was trying to use both feet.

It didn't take much to realize that, even at a very early age, he had a special talent for playing the game. It was a daunting feeling for me – I knew he had been given an extraordinary gift and it was my job to try and bring it out. It wasn't long before that job took over my life.

It was at a team called Kingfisher that David got his first taste of organized football. They played in a local Sunday league and I'd joined them not long after we moved back to Chingford, when David was about four. I was a nippy right-winger but I didn't have quite the skill my son has been blessed with. And, to be honest, my career was pretty much coming to an end as David's was beginning.

I know he's said I gave up football to concentrate on coaching him but I was starting to get a few aches and pains so I knew I didn't have long to go as a player. The fact that David was showing so much promise made it much easier for me to do that.

My son's football took me over and it was a great substitution.

I think any dad would have done the same. I just wanted my son to play as well as he could and fulfil the potential I could see he had. I admit I pushed him – but I'm sure he wanted to be pushed. He had the passion to succeed and all I did was tap into that and make it happen.

Kingfisher used to train on a Thursday evening at a place called Wadham Lodge, a couple of miles from our home. There were three or four pitches there and a small clubhouse, with a bar overlooking the main pitch. David always used to come with me, even when he was very small. I really enjoyed having him with me.

We spent hours working in the park and at Wadham Lodge in all weathers. It didn't matter if it was raining or cold, we would be out there. Sunday mornings were the best time – we would go out and spend hours practising together, working on technique and going through drill after drill.

Sometimes, I'd get him to go to the halfway line and start dribbling from there. He had to pretend there were players on the pitch and that he had to beat them before firing in a shot. If the shot wasn't on target, I'd get him to do it again.

Then I'd get him going down the wing, dribbling the ball. I'd stand on the penalty spot and say, 'I want you to cross it into my arms. I'll give you a yard either side but if you can get in my arms, great.' Nine times out of ten, he'd hit me.

If he couldn't get it first off, I'd make him do it again and again until he got it right, first with his right foot and then with his left. But he wanted to know how to do things properly – he wanted to learn. I was teaching him how to kick a ball and making sure he got the basics right from the very start. I think that has served him well throughout his career.

I would also stand on the centre spot and put a ball three or four yards in front of me; he would have to curl it round me and he had to do it on both sides of me, using first the inside and then outside of his foot – then he'd switch and do it with the other foot.

I'd stand in line with the post and get him to take a free-kick from directly in front of me. He had to curl it round me and into the goal. It was a great drill and you can see how all that has paid off for him now.

Other times, I would stand in front of the post and he would stand in front of me with the ball. And I would say: 'Right, I want you to hit the post.'

Then he had to stand further away and curl the ball in. I'd show him how to do it, show him which part of the foot to hit the ball with, and he'd try to copy me. We used to train like that. I'd tell him: 'Right, now try one with the side of your foot; now try it with the top of your foot.' And he'd work and work until he got it right, even at such a young age.

I'd go in goal and we'd use a full-size ball. I'd roll it out to him and say: 'Go on, hit it as hard as you can.' First, I'd get him to sidefoot it, and then I'd throw it in the air and get him to volley it. Right from an early age, he could volley a ball – at the age of six he was volleying a ball as well as most 12-year-olds.

Then we'd work on kicking a dead ball. He was always fantastic at that. He had such a hard shot and he could take a corner on a full-size pitch and get it into the middle.

Time after time, hour after hour, we would go through the same routines. That constant practice may sound like hard work to some people, but we both really enjoyed it. It was great for me to see how he developed and I used to get such a thrill from watching him perfect a particular skill.

He listened and he got it right. What you see him do now is what we used to do back then. The curling free-kicks, the long passes hit exactly to the right place, the pinpoint crosses from out wide – we practised all of that.

It sounds incredible, but people would stop and watch him practise, even when he was very young. If we were having a kickaround at lunchtime on a Sunday, people would be looking out of the windows of the local bar. Then we'd go up for a drink and everyone would be singing his praises. It made me very proud.

I admit I was pretty hard on him. I pushed him to make the best of himself, to develop the fantastic talent he had. If I didn't think he was trying, I'd say, 'Do it again, you're not doing it.'

'Oh, Dad,' he'd moan, 'I'm fed up with all this. I want to go upstairs and play pool.'

'No, not until you get this right,' I'd say. 'If you do it right, we'll go up and get a drink.'

I wasn't one to mollycoddle him and I never minced my words with him. I was always the one that told him off and I probably did go a bit over the top sometimes.

His mum used to say to me: 'Why don't you leave him alone? Don't be so hard on him.'

But I wasn't a dad who would put my arm around him and tell him he'd done well if he hadn't.

When we went over the park, if he couldn't do something, we'd stay out there until he could do it. Take his crosses, for instance – he's noted for those now, but in the park I made him do them over and over again until he got them right. I wanted everything done perfectly.

One time we were out there and I was trying to get him to run down the wing and then cross the ball into my arms standing on the penalty spot. He just couldn't do it that day and after practising it time after time and not getting it right he said to me, 'Oh, Dad, I've had enough. Can't we go in?'

'No, not until you get it right. I don't care how long we spend out here and we'll keep going so long you won't have any dinner unless you get it.'

I'd get him to do it, say, eight times in a row to prove he'd really got it. One or two could just be luck. I was a bit easier on him with his left foot but it was so important for him to do it properly.

Some lads respond to a clip round the ear but David was never like that. I could get under his skin by having a dig at him but, when he'd done well, I always knew it was important to give him a hug and give him some praise.

I also used to play for a summer league side called Griffin and we used to travel all over London for games. They were usually on Wednesday nights and David always came too.

On match nights, I'd always make sure I was home early and David would be waiting for me, sitting on the front step in his United kit, with boots on ready to go.

As soon as I walked up the path, he'd be saying: 'Come on, Dad, hurry up. We don't want to be late, do we?'

We'd always try to get to the ground early to have a kickabout and that was really where I started to teach him the basics. You couldn't really call it coaching but I always thought there was no point going out on the pitch and learning things if you weren't going to learn them properly.

David would have been about five or six at the time. I used to get him to stand on the edge of the penalty area and say to him: '50p for every time you can hit the crossbar.'

It cost me a fortune. Even at that age, he could do that – it was incredible.

To make it harder, I'd move him forward but he'd still hit the bar more often than not. I spent a lot of time with him but the amazing thing was that he really wanted to learn. He was such a good listener and that was true right the way through his childhood. He always wanted to work and he always wanted to learn.

I remember one game we played over at Walthamstow in the summer league. David and I arrived at about 5.30pm for a 7pm kick-off. So by the time I'd got changed and out on the pitch, we had about an hour to practise before the game.

David and I went through a few of the drills but as the kick-off got nearer, it was clear we were going to be short of players. I think we ended up playing with only nine men, so it turned out to be a really tough game and I was completely knackered by the end of it.

As I walked off the pitch I could see David over on the next pitch. He'd spent the whole of our game playing with a few of the other lads but as soon as he saw me, he said: 'Come on, Dad – you go in goal and we'll practise shooting.'

This was about the last thing I wanted to hear, but what could I do? By this time it was approaching 9pm, but we stayed out there until it was too dark to see, just practising, practising and practising. I hadn't even had a drink.

Of course, when we got home his mum was furious. 'Where've you been all this time? It's gone eleven o'clock.'

'It's not me,' I said, 'it's him! He wouldn't let me come home.'

And it was true. He just wanted to be out there the whole time. I can never recall a time when he didn't want to be on a football pitch.

He would spend hours practising on the patio, kicking the ball up against the wall and controlling it instantly, keeping it on his neck, letting it hit his chest, then his head, his thighs. Hour after hour, he'd go through his routines.

Even at that age, people were starting to notice David as a good player. I remember watching him at school and hearing other parents say, 'Look at that little boy, can't he kick a ball?'

He went on a summer skills course organized by some former Tottenham players – Cliff Jones, Roger and Ian Morgan, Jimmy Neighbour – and he just left everybody amazed. It was just over the road from the Spurs ground and David's ability really stood out.

The course involved doing things like dribbling, shooting, heading, control, chipping the ball to targets and he was awarded the top badge at the age of six. There were kids there of 15 and 16 who couldn't do the things he was doing.

They used to organize games at the end of the courses and even at that age David would go in with much older boys and more than hold his own. It was thrilling to watch.

I never had any doubts about his talent. I can't say that I knew he would end up as a professional but you couldn't help comparing him with the other lads of his age. And when you saw him up against them, you knew he had something special.

I must admit I ended up trying to organize my work around our football. If I knew there was a game on, or a chance to get over the park with David, I'd do anything to get home early but if Sandra told me we had to go out, I wasn't all that bothered if I made it home or not!

The one worry we did have was his size – there was just nothing of him. He was always quite skinny and short for his age. Throughout his childhood, there was this nagging doubt that he wouldn't grow big enough to make it into the pro ranks.

What he lacked in size, he more than made up for in courage though. Sometimes when we went training, he'd ask to join in with my mates. We're talking big lads – fully grown men. And a couple of times I said: 'All right, come on then. But whatever you do, don't keep hold of the ball because if you do, you're going to get clumped and knocked over.'

Well, two or three times he did get knocked over. And two or three times he came off the pitch crying. And I just said, 'See what I mean?' But that was good for him; another dad might have said, 'Oh, come on, son. Go and sit over there and sit this one out.' But they'd never learn from that. I used to say to him: 'That's what I told you. You get the ball and your control is always so important. Get it down, look up and get it away. If you've got to control it and the ball rolls off and you have to control it again, you've lost that vital time and space – and given your opponent a chance to get to you.'

That's where he learned about the importance of controlling the ball and passing it off quickly. I showed him how crucial it was to get a ball and stop it with one touch, which gives you two or three seconds to look around and make a pass. If you don't and you've got to take your time, you're going to get clumped.

He was quicker than many of the bigger lads. He used to lay it off quickly and go and find space. As he got to train with us more and more, they'd be looking to give him the ball because he was so good. At first, they'd think, 'Oh, yeah, little kid, we'll soon sort him out.' But when they saw what he could do, he earned their respect and pretty soon they were treating him as one of them.

And he was a fast learner – he understood quickly that if he released the ball and found space, he'd get the ball back.

The worst thing with David was trying to get him out of the park and off the football pitch of an evening. We were quite strict about all the children's bedtimes so when David was about seven or eight it would get to about 8pm and I'd be sent over to the park to bring him home.

Of course, he never wanted to come and he could always persuade me just to have one more shot or one more corner. His mum would go mad when we got home but football always came first.

The biggest punishment we could give him was to stop him going out to play football – and that was the only one he took seriously. We used to threaten him with not going but that used to affect me and my enjoyment, so we always gave in and let him go.

I don't suppose that approach figures in many of the modern guides to parenting but I don't think it did David any harm.

It's been incredible watching him develop over the years – a complete pleasure and never a chore. It is wonderful to think of what he has achieved having started from such humble beginnings.

Now, when I stand in Real Madrid's Bernabeu Stadium and watch him training I think back to those days at Chase Lane Park and Wadham Lodge. Out on the pitch, my son is hitting 50-yard passes to Brazilian World Cup winner Roberto Carlos and they are all inch perfect – just as they used to be to me on those cold winter days in Chingford.

FROM RIDGEWAY ROVERS TO OLD TRAFFORD 1982-1989

'David would never have been a footballer without Ridgeway Rovers. He joined them when they started and the people there were vital in making him the player he is today.'

He was about seven and I'd been thinking he needed to join a team for some time. He was clearly talented but he needed more than I could give him on my own to really bring that talent out. I'd looked around at a few local clubs but none of them really seemed right for David.

I knew the most important thing was the coaching – and you only get good coaching from good coaches. It's always hard to tell how talented someone is until you've seen them working, so I was more than a little suspicious when David came back from Chase Lane Park one night all excited, saying: 'Dad, Dad, there's a man over the park wants me to join his club.'

David seemed so thrilled that someone had asked him to join a team. My instinct was to say no but the more he went on about it, the more I thought I should check it out. A few nights later I went over to the park with David and saw a huge burly bloke I didn't recognize going through a few simple routines with about 40 kids.

'That's him, Dad … Go and speak to him, go on,' urged David. He was like a dog with a bone, especially when it came to football, so it wasn't long before I was chatting to the coach, Stuart Underwood.

He was 6ft 4in and had played at senior amateur level with Walthamstow Avenue. He was a bit of a sergeant major type – very disciplined, very regimented. I could tell from the moment I met him he wouldn't take any nonsense. I think a lot of the kids were a little scared of him at first but that was no bad thing. When he spoke, they listened and they all seemed to respect him. I warmed to Stuart straight away. We were on the same wavelength and the way he treated the kids was exactly the way I thought they should be treated.

He was brilliant with the boys – he knew which ones he could shout at, which ones he could soft talk and which ones needed an arm round the shoulder. He gave them all encouragement and discipline, just as I had been doing with David.

Stuart, who was a foreman at Hawker Siddeley in Walthamstow, really had a vision of where he wanted Ridgeway to go and what he wanted it to become. A club in which the boys learned all the basic skills of football, but also learned how to conduct themselves well. The idea was that they would have fun but also that there would be enough discipline to mould them in the right way and keep them out of trouble.

As I chatted away to him, I started to get really enthusiastic about his plans. By the end of that first conversation, I'd offered to help coach the kids with him. Of course, part of the reason for that was to keep an eye on David but I was also picking up on Stuart's passion and was fired with the belief that we could really create something that would stand all the kids in good stead.

Not long after, another one of the dads, Steve Kirby, came in as a coach and together the three of us started the club that would play such a big part in all our lives for the next five or six years.

It was one of the best things I ever did. I was still playing my Sunday football at the time but I packed that in not long after to concentrate on David and Ridgeway.

We started off by having trials and we whittled the 40 kids down to 22 or 23, including David of course. It was great to watch them at first, like a load of ants all swarming around the ball, desperate for a touch and hardly ever passing.

We used to train once a week, either at the nearby Wellington School, where we could work in the gym, or at Kelmscott, a local sports centre with a playing field.

Stuart and Steve, who was a carpenter by trade, used to do most of the technique coaching – I used to take the boys jogging round the field to get them warmed up. Then the three of us would get together and split the boys up into small groups. We made a pretty good team. Of course, we had a few arguments along the way but we all had the boys' best interests at heart and we always managed to sort things out.

The kids couldn't play competitive matches until they were ten years old but we started off with a few friendlies against local teams. We told the lads the score didn't matter, that the important thing was learning the right habits and doing the right things but pretty soon they started winning games. And not just winning them 1–0 or 2–0, but 10–0 and 12–0.

We were lucky to have such a talented group of lads to work with. Besides David, there was Micah Hyde, who's now at Watford; Jason Brissett, who had a pro career with Bournemouth; Ryan Kirby, who was at Doncaster; and Chris Day who was a centre-forward for Ridgeway but ended up as a goalkeeper with QPR. We always prided ourselves on getting the best out of all the boys, even those who didn't have as much talent as the better ones, and it really worked for us.

Like David, a lot of the Ridgeway lads went to Chingford High and played over at Chase Lane Park. There was a whole crowd of them, including David, Ryan, Nicky Lockwood, Danny Fielder, Richie and Glenn Sutton, Stuart Underwood's son Robert, who all lived locally so they really got to know each other well. They trained together with Ridgeway but they also seemed to spend every evening at the park, playing makeshift games against whoever happened to be over there.

It was a great environment for any young lad to grow up in. They all looked out for each other and their shared love of football kept them out of trouble. David made some great friends among those lads, although he's obviously drifted away from them in recent years.

Slowly they started to play properly, holding their positions, passing the ball around and creating moves between themselves. It was fantastic to watch and I have to admit I was really thrilled at the way things went. Sandra and I both got more and more involved and football really began to take over both our lives.

Sandra was one of the few mums who could drive so whenever I was working and David had a game or training session, she stepped in. David has said she probably spent as much time as I did on his football and he's not wrong. When your son gets into something in as big a way as David got into football, any parent would put themselves out and we were no different.

Stuart insisted that whenever we travelled away, all the boys had to wear team jumpers, with the crest and team name embroidered on the front. And they always had to wear ties – he was a stickler for us being turned out immaculately. Of course, that was no problem for David because he always loved being smart but that wasn't the case for all the boys.

Stuart also insisted on all the boys having completely clean kit, right down to the boots. I remember one lad turning up for a game on a Sunday with boots still filthy from the game he'd played the day before and Stuart wouldn't let him play. He said: 'I'm not having that. You clean them up before you come here. There's no excuse.' This poor lad ended up washing his boots under the tap and Stuart eventually let him on for the second half.

I always made sure David's boots were spotless before training or matches at Ridgeway. Every week, I'd be the one scrubbing off all the mud and then getting out the polish. I made sure they were immaculate, but still David liked to take the mickey.

He'd always say: 'Have you done my boots yet, Dad?'

'You cheeky little…' I'd reply. 'Clean 'em yourself.'

'Oi, Dad, you've missed a bit. I can't wear them like that.'

If we ever reached it to a semi-final or a final Stuart would organize a team bus, to make sure we all turned up together and looked like a real team. As soon as we arrived, we'd go out on the pitch for a look around and to get a feel of the turf, just like the pros do. Then we'd go into the dressing room, have a team talk and get all the kit laid out properly for them.

Right from the start, we tried to make it as professional a set-up as possible and I'm sure that paid off. It certainly did for David. It showed him how important it was to be properly prepared and it gave him the perfect start for a pro career.

Of course, getting all those jumpers and all that kit cost money and none of the parents was all that well-off. But we used to organize loads of fund-raising events, discos, dances and raffles, that sort of thing. All the parents would muck in to do the food, buy the drink and sell the tickets – anything to make sure our boys had the best.

One of the dads used to work on Smithfield meat market so each week he'd come with a joint of beef or some steak and he'd go around the touchline raffling it. He'd sell tickets to the Ridgeway parents and those from the opposition and someone would walk off with something for Sunday lunch!

David loved it from the word go. I think he really felt at home in that kind of football environment and adored being part of the team. He always wanted to be involved and he took it very seriously.

I remember when he was about eight and we were going down to Camber Sands for a week's holiday. I had deliberately organized it for a week when Ridgeway weren't playing but Stuart suddenly organized a game at the last minute. Well, all hell broke loose when David found out he'd have to miss the game.

'I'm not going on holiday,' he said. 'You can all go without me. I'm not missing this game, I don't care what anyone says.'

Like I say, he could be stubborn at times.

We tried to talk him out of it. 'Missing one game won't hurt. Don't worry, just come on holiday and forget about football for a while.'

But he wouldn't have it. He just said, 'I want to play and that's it. I'm not going to miss it.'

So we reached a compromise – we went on holiday but came back a day early so he could play in the game. Of course, his sisters weren't all that pleased but we couldn't stop David playing his football.

Stuart was excellent at building the boys' confidence, even if I didn't always agree with his methods.

I remember one training session in which Stuart was having a real go at David. I don't think it was anything specific – he'd just decided David was going to get it that particular week. David probably wasn't trying hard enough or not taking it seriously. Perhaps David wasn't sharp enough for him. I don't know, but all I could hear was Stuart having a go. I just got more and more annoyed and eventually I snapped.

'Come on, David,' I shouted. 'We're going home. I ain't having this … Come on, get in the car.'

Stuart just shouted to David, 'Stay where you are.'

That just made me even more furious but as I marched towards them, Stuart walked towards me and pulled me aside. 'Look, Ted, don't do anything stupid. I'm only trying to bring out the best in him. I know he can do better and I just want to help him.'

I knew what he was getting at and, in my heart, I probably agreed with him. But I didn't like him having a go at my son in public like that. I thought it was something that should have been said privately. I suppose it was to all our credit that something like that could blow up and then be over with almost as soon as it had started. I swallowed my pride, we shook hands and went back to the session. We just got on with it.

Steve Kirby was the joker in our pack. He was always having a laugh and the boys really thought the world of him. If Stuart was like a headmaster, then Steve was like a big brother to them.

I remember one Christmas we'd gone out for a meal as a big group. All the boys and all their families – about 40 or 50 of us had gone to the Hall Tavern, a pub just up the road from where I live.

I have to say most of the dads just got blotto and Steve had gone further than most. He was so drunk it was untrue – he got all the tinsel off the Christmas tree and put it in his hair and round his shoulders and was dancing round the room like a lunatic. The boys thought it was hysterical and all the parents joined in the fun.

We never made a man of the match award at Ridgeway, which was quite unusual at the time. We always thought it was unfair to pick out one boy for special praise when two or three might have done well in a game. We saved our awards for the end of the season – most improved player, players' player, the manager's player. We got the boys to write down the player they wanted to get their award and we ran it absolutely fairly.

I watched just about every match David played for Ridgeway, so much so that the ones I didn't see almost stick in my mind more.

One weekend I had to do an emergency job at Langan's, the famous London restaurant. The money was so good I couldn't afford to turn it down. I was with another couple of lads and had already told them I wouldn't be able to work on the Sunday morning because of David's football. But by the time we went home on Saturday night, I knew they wouldn't finish on time if I went.

So I went in to help them – but I was no use because all I could think about was David's football. It was really winding me up and I kept looking at my watch, imagining what they would be doing: 9.30am – leaving the house for the game; 10am – arriving at the ground and getting changed; 11am – kicking off. I wondered what the score was, wondered how David was getting on, wondered if he'd scored.

The morning seemed to go on for ever and this was long before the days of mobile phones so I couldn't get any updates on the score. It was a nightmare, so I resolved there and then not to miss any more games.

It was about this time that I decided to set up my own company. I left Benham's and started up with a friend of mine before going it alone in 1987. I was lucky enough to get the contract to maintain all the gas cookers at the Park Lane Hotel, largely thanks to the then head chef, Nigel Frost, who's still a great friend of mine. From there, I've never looked back.

That made it a lot easier to work my life around David's football. I didn't have to answer to anyone except myself, so I could see all the games I wanted. Looking back, I can see just how much I gave up to help him – I sacrificed my work, my free time and a lot of money to follow his football. But it was more than a fair swap – I've had so much pleasure in watching him achieve his ambitions.

Ridgeway went from strength to strength, with David playing right wing and scoring quite a few goals along the way. We won both the County League and the County Cup and once went 92 games without getting beaten – an incredible achievement at any level of football.

I remember the day that run came to an end – we lost 2–1 to Enfield Rangers, having totally dominated the game but never being able to get the equalizer. Back in the dressing room, the whole team was in tears, including David. I'd never seen anything like it, but that was how much it meant to them. They had been desperate to get to 100 games unbeaten and were distraught at finally losing. Of course, the next week, they went out and won 16–0.

But even though David was playing in such a successful side, he could still have his off days. I remember one game when he was terrible – passes were going astray, he wasn't trying, he just wasn't up for it.

After the final whistle, I didn't hesitate to tell him what I thought. 'David, why did you play like that? You were rubbish today and I know you could have played better.'

As I was having a go at him, the tears welled up in his eyes and then started to trickle down his cheeks. That was when I knew I'd hit home. He hated crying in front of anyone, so to do it in front of his team-mates showed how hurt he was.

'Oh, leave him alone,' said Sandra. 'Don't be so hard on him.'

'No, he's not doing what I want him to do,' I replied. 'And he's got to learn.'

If he did well, I'd just put my arm around him or give him a wink. That was all that was needed. But if he didn't play well, I'd be brutally honest with him; I'd say, 'David, you were crap today.'

Some of the dads would say to their boys after every game, 'Oh, you played really well today – best one on the pitch.' But I always believed that if you give kids a lot of praise then they have nothing to work for. If David had played well, I'd tell him he'd had a good game and then say, 'But what about the silly ball you played down the line – why couldn't you have played it inside?'

We were always looking to improve and even though he used to go into his shell sometimes, he never got furious with me. He'd just go quiet and I'd know he wasn't happy. But he would think about what I'd said and then, maybe a couple of weeks later, he'd do something in a game that showed me he'd taken it on board.

I know I was hard – but I was right. Where he is now is where we – not only me, but David as well – wanted him to be. He did it but we worked as a team. He's a great worker – a bit of a sulker, but a great worker.

Some people might think that's being too hard or too nasty but you only have to look at where my son is today to realize I did the right thing. I'm so pleased at how he's turned out and without that bit of roughness I don't think he'd be there.

If you keep telling kids how great they are, then they have nothing to strive for. But if you show them how much better they could be, they have something to work towards.

Sometimes I'd point out his mistakes and he'd try to explain why he'd chosen to do something. We'd get home and he'd go up for a bath but I could tell he was thinking about what I'd said. He'd come down later and say: 'Dad, you were right, you know.'

Then he'd say to me, 'Come on, Dad – what do you want to watch on the telly?' And we'd put the football on, or dig out a video of an old game and sit together and watch it.

But even then, I'd get him to watch specific players to see what they did, why they did it and how they did it.

Mind you, that would almost always end up in a bit of a wrestling match. We usually sat on the floor together to watch football. As often as not, we'd end up digging one another in the ribs or mucking up each other's hair and then it would develop into a full-scale fun fight. It was great – the kind of thing that makes a father feel really close to his son.

It wasn't long before Ridgeway's reputation started to spread and the first scouts began turning up at our games.

West Ham were the first professional club to reveal their interest in David. We were playing over at Tottenham and I spotted this chap who I'd seen at a few games before. Eventually, he sidled up to me and started chatting. He soon revealed who he was and said the Hammers wanted David, who was ten at the time, down for a trial.

Ironically enough, just a couple of weeks earlier Stuart had called all the Ridgeway dads together and warned us that there were a lot of scouts about. But he urged us not to go to pro clubs. His advice was very much to let the boys enjoy their football and if they were good enough, the clubs would come back.

I must admit, Sandra and I thought twice about what to do, just as any parents would. We went over to Upton Park with David to watch a game and were tempted by the chance to join a top club. But in the end, we decided it would have been too much for him.

He was training twice a week with Ridgeway and playing for them; he was also playing for his primary school and we just thought it was a heck of a lot of football for a young lad. And we trusted Stuart when he said the pro clubs would be back.

Of course, he was right. Almost every time we played there would be a scout or two there and they'd be trying to get to know us, chatting to us and asking a few questions about the games, the boys and so on. Nothing too heavy at the time – they were just laying the groundwork for later on.

Eventually, when David was coming up to his eleventh birthday, we decided it was time for him to join a pro club – the question was, which one? If he'd had his way, it would have been United but that would have meant moving north and we just couldn't do that at the time. Clubs like West Ham and Leyton Orient were interested but, in the end, it came down to a choice between Tottenham and Arsenal, the two north London giants.

He had done some training at both clubs, at Arsenal under Pat Rice, who's now Arsene Wenger's assistant/first-team coach, and at Spurs, where David Pleat was the manager. The coaching at both clubs was fantastic and he just couldn't decide. We asked around among other parents but there was really nothing to choose. So Sandra said the only way to choose was to put both names in a bag and pick one out, which was exactly what we did.

And that's how he ended up as a schoolboy at Spurs. His granddad was delighted but I shudder to think what might have happened if he'd pulled out Arsenal!

Tottenham were superb for him and looked after him really well. He trained with them once a week and was there with Sol

Campbell, who is now his England colleague and has enjoyed a fantastic career at Spurs and Arsenal, and Nicky Barmby, who played for Spurs, Liverpool and England.

Even then, David insisted on wearing his Manchester United strip for the Tottenham training sessions. He used to take a lot of stick for that but there was never any doubt where his loyalty lay.

It was about this time that David first went up to Manchester United. Sandra had seen a piece about the Bobby Charlton Summer School on the children's TV programme, *Blue Peter*. The school offered a week-long soccer skills course in the summer holidays to kids aged ten and over. Of course, as soon as David heard about it he was desperate to go. It cost about £130 – money we didn't have – but his granddad paid for it and I think it's an investment that's paid off.

David was still only ten and he had to go up to Manchester for the week on his own. He stayed in Manchester University's halls of residence, living with the other boys on the course and very much fending for himself. It was quite a daunting thing for any young boy to do and David was one of the youngest there.

Sandra and I went up to spend that week with my brother John, his wife Sue and their two children, Michael and Katie, who live in Southport near Liverpool. But even though we were quite close by, it still felt like we were a million miles away from David.

We used to phone him every day and he kept saying how much he was enjoying it and how good it was but we could tell from his voice that he was finding it hard being on his own.

Then we rang him on the Wednesday night.

'Hi, son, how are you?'

'Not too good, Dad – I've got toothache. It's pretty bad. Can you come over?'

We felt pretty miserable to think of our little boy a long way from home and in pain. We shot straight over to be with him and give him a bit of moral support. I think any parent would have done the

Football & Athletic Co. Ltd.
MEMBERS OF FOOTBALL ASSOCIATION AND THE FOOTBALL LEAGUE

748 High Road, Tottenham N17 0AP. Telephone 01-808 8080 Telex 295261 Fax 01-885 1951

Ticket Office: 01-801 3323   Dial - A - Seat: 01-808 3030   Ansaphone: 01-808 1020

Our Ref: KW/ija

20th April 1989

Dear

re: UNDER 15 TRAINING WEEK - MONDAY 7th - FRIDAY 11th AUGUST
     10am - 12.30 pm AT METAL BOX

You are invited to attend our training week as above. Please bring your
training kit, boots and a towel.

The U 15 squad will be required to train on Tuesdays and Thursdays thereafter,
and to play on Sunday mornings on a regular basis.

We hope you have an enjoyable summer and look forward to seeing you next season.

Best wishes.

K. Waldon.

K WALDON
YOUTH TEAM MANAGER

League Champions
1951   1961
League Cup Winners
1971   1973

Winners of the "Double" F.A. Cup and League Championship 1960-61
"The European Cup Winners Cup" 1962-63 & the "U.E.F.A. Cup" 1971-72 & 1983-84
Registered Office: 748 High Road, Tottenham, London N170AP
Registered Number: 57186 England.

Winners of F.A. Cup
1901, 1921, 1961, 1962
1967, 1981, 1982

When it was time for David to join a pro club, we eventually decided on
Tottenham, one of the north London giants, where he trained once a week.

same. Of course, by the time we'd got there, he said the toothache had gone!

We spoke to the woman running the place and she said she thought he was just a little bit homesick. So we stayed with him for a few hours and talked him round. And he seemed to be OK, so we left. And when we spoke to him later, he said the toothache had come back a bit but he thought he'd be all right.

That same week, David rang us again and sounded really excited.

'Dad, they're doing a tour of Old Trafford. Do you and Uncle John want to come?'

I couldn't believe it. Even though I'd supported United all my life, I'd never been on the tour of the ground before. It was like being let into heaven – but even then, I never dared let myself believe my son could one day play for this fantastic club.

I'm not sure who was more impressed on that tour – me or David. It was wonderful to see the changing rooms, the boardroom and the trophy room. We were both gobsmacked to see how magnificent everything was. It really brought home to us just how massive a club United was.

On the Saturday, all the parents turned up for the prizegiving. Bobby Charlton, the player I'd idolized all my life, was there and he said how good the kids had been. He shook all the parents' hands and, without referring directly to David, he said he knew a couple of them had been very homesick and had been struggling. But he said they'd be a lot better for having come through it – and he was right.

We had no idea at that time that United thought anything special of David. They never said anything to us – it was far more that United made a massive impression on David.

Despite all the homesickness and the fact that he hadn't won anything, he spent the whole journey home telling us what a fantastic week he'd had and how much he wanted to go back next year. A lot of kids would have remembered the homesickness and never wanted to go back, but David's love of football was more important than any worries about missing Mum and Dad.

Of course, he did go back a year later in 1986 and ended up as the overall winner of his week. I think that really put him on the map as far as United were concerned.

As a winner, he was through to the final in December, where he would be up against the winners from all the other weeks of the summer school. I think about 6500 boys from across Britain and Ireland started out so just to reach the final was quite an achievement.

For the final, United paid for us to come up and stay at the Portland Hotel. The first part was to be held at United's old training ground, The Cliff, in Salford, with the second part at Old Trafford just before the start of United's League game against Tottenham.

On the morning of the final, we had trouble getting him up. He was so relaxed he just wanted to sleep and sleep. But when he finally came round, the nerves kicked in. Every five minutes, he was off to the toilet – a sure sign he was feeling the pressure.

When we left the hotel, I just put my arm round him and said, 'Go on, son – do your best.' I gave him a kiss and he got on the coach. His mum and I waved him goodbye.

We went to watch the final and I was amazed to see the tests featured all the stuff we'd been doing for hour after hour over at Chase Lane Park, at Wadham Lodge and with Ridgeway – keepy-ups, dribbling round cones, sprinting and shooting, one-touch football.

David was incredible – I wouldn't say he was showing off but he really turned it on. They ended up playing a little game and he was putting the ball through the other lads' legs and all his tricks were coming off. It was great to watch and I couldn't have been more proud.

It wasn't that he was being big-headed – it was just that somehow he knew he needed to make a good impression. But he was doing so many tricks, it was as if he were saying: 'I'm here. This is where I belong.' That's something he can still do today – if he needs a massive performance he can somehow produce it, even if his team isn't doing all that well. Just remember the goal he scored against Greece at Old Trafford to get England to the European Championships in 2004.

I remember one of the coaches' wives came up to me during the final and asked, 'Is that your lad, there, the little blond kid?'

'Yes,' I replied cautiously, a little worried he might have done something wrong.

'Oh, he's fantastic,' she beamed. 'They're all talking about him. I've never seen anything like it. He's absolutely brilliant.' Of course, the old chest puffed out and I was so proud.

I think he was well in the lead by the time they broke for lunch. I had a quick word with him as they walked off the pitch but the last thing he wanted to talk about was his own performance – all he wanted to know was how Ridgeway were getting on in a Cup game they were playing that day. Luckily enough, they won but I can't say that bothered me too much at the time: my mind was firmly on how David was getting on.

Sandra and I were taken off to have lunch with the other parents but we were so nervous we couldn't eat. Then we were driven to Old Trafford to watch the last few tests of the final and the game against Spurs.

Watching him walk on to the pitch at the greatest stadium in the world for the first time is still one of my most enduring memories. He looked so tiny and the stadium seemed so enormous around him. I really thought my heart would burst with pride.

All the boys were introduced to the crowd and when the announcer said: 'David Beckham from Leytonstone,' a huge roar went up from the Spurs fans. Then the announcer said: 'And David is a massive United fan.' Of course, all the Tottenham cheers turned to jeers, while the Old Trafford fans yelled their support.

The final was unbelievably nerve-wracking for me and Sandra but David seemed to take it in his stride. Once the football was underway, the nerves didn't affect him, even though there were probably about 40,000 people in the stadium by then. He had to do a few more tests there, again all the things we'd been practising for years, like dribbling, shooting, long passing and chipping balls to a target.

They did a few more tests at half-time, then all of a sudden I saw a photographer pull David aside, along with one of the coaches.

We couldn't work out what was going on, but we didn't think much more of it once the second half had started. Then, about 10 or 15 minutes before the end of the game, one of the officials came up to us in the stand and called us over. He just said: 'I'm delighted to tell you that David has won. Many congratulations.'

We couldn't believe it. I was utterly stunned, I couldn't speak and it was like I was gasping for air. We went through to the presentation and everyone seemed to be there. David had come up from the dressing rooms, all showered and changed, to stand beside us. And there was Bobby Charlton, my all-time hero, about to present my son with the top award.

It was an incredible feeling and I still struggle to remember much of what was said in that presentation. Of course, Bobby made a lovely speech and was full of praise for all the boys but he did make a special mention of David. Everyone was coming up to us and congratulating us, saying how well David had done. We were immensely proud but I noticed David slink away to get near a television set so he could watch the United–Spurs game.

When we got back to the hotel, none of us could settle down. We had a meal together and then tried to go to bed but we couldn't sleep after a day like that. We were all buzzing. David still gets hyper after games now and it takes him a long time to calm down – back then it was even worse.

His prize for winning was a two-week trip to train with Barcelona, who were then managed by Terry Venables and could boast such stars as Gary Lineker, Mark Hughes, Steve Archibald and Bernd Schuster. He went out there with the two lads who'd finished second and third and a coach from the Bobby Charlton soccer school, Ray Whelan.

Mind you, even then David knew where his priorities lay. Ridgeway were in a Cup Final at White Hart Lane on the middle Saturday of the fortnight and David insisted on flying home to play in it. His granddad, the massive Spurs fan, was happy to fork out for a return flight so he could see David play at his beloved White Hart Lane. Ridgeway lost that game 2–1 and then David was back on the plane on his own for the second week in Barcelona.

By this time, David had just started at secondary school, Chingford High, which everyone called the Nevin because it was in Nevin Road. He really seemed to enjoy his new school, if only because it was another football team to play for. He went straight into the school team and it wasn't long before he was playing district football for Waltham Forest and then county for Essex.

Football was still far and away the most important thing in his life and I have to admit his schoolwork suffered. He was never going to be an academic genius but his reports from the Nevin make it clear he indulged in a fair bit of mischief-making and mucking about in class, often to the irritation of his teachers:

July 1987

A rather worrying set of reports. There is obviously concern at David's lack of effort, concentration and homework. He must try hard to improve these if he is to make progress. David is a pleasant and helpful pupil.
K Thompson, form tutor

July 1987
David has ability but he finds it difficult to concentrate on
his work. His tendancy [sic] to chat and giggle in class has
seriously impeded his progress.
C Dunlea, Humanities

May 1988
David is a most pleasant boy who always gives his best.
However he has missed rather too many lessons due to his
injuries. Perhaps a little less football would help.
Martin Felden, PE

December 1990
David must try a little harder – at present all his eggs are in
one basket. A valuable member of the football team.
John Bulloch, year tutor

Despite those reports, he never bunked off school or missed any time unless he was ill. He may not have been perfectly behaved but he loved going to school. I think he just enjoyed being with all his mates, plus he always had someone to play football with at break times.

David's one passion at school outside football was drawing. Cartoon characters were probably his speciality and he used to spend hours on them. But if you look through his old books, you can see from the doodles of footballs and players that he was thinking about the game all the time.

People often ask me whether David really was so perfect as a child but I can honestly say that he never looked for trouble and never got into scrapes at school. He sometimes got into trouble for talking in class or mucking about at the back and he used to chuck a few rubbers. He was a bit of a chatterbox and I know he didn't do his homework as well as he should have done but that was the worst you could say of him.

When we went to open nights it was always the same message – he sometimes mucks about in class and he could do a lot better. I'm sure that was true but there was only ever one thing on his mind – football, football and more football. He'd never want to sit in with his books, he just wanted to be out there playing.

It was around this time that United's interest really stepped up. Of course, they'd seen what he could do at the Bobby Charlton summer schools but David never thought he'd be spotted properly. In fact, he used to moan about living in the south because he thought United would only look for boys in the northwest of England. I wouldn't say he'd given up hope of playing for United but he always thought he'd have more of a chance at Spurs or Arsenal.

But David didn't know about a man called Malcolm Fidgeon, who was to become a great friend of the family and was a key figure in making David the player he is today.

The first time he approached us was at one of David's few matches I missed. David was playing over in Woodford and Sandra had taken him because I was working. At the end of the game, Sandra was hanging around waiting for him to come out of the changing room. He was always the last one out and it was a standing joke that he would take longer than anyone else to shower and dress. Anyway, as Sandra stood in the car park Malcolm came up and introduced himself.

'Mrs Beckham? I'm the London scout for Manchester United and I've been watching your son for some time,' he said. 'We'd like him to come up to Manchester for a trial. We think he's got potential and we'd like some of our coaches up at Old Trafford to have a look at him.'

Sandra was flabbergasted and didn't know what to say. She couldn't believe what he'd said and it took a while to really sink in. She ended up giving him our number and telling him to speak to me later on. She was as nervous as anything and just wanted time to think.

As soon as David came out of the changing room Sandra told him about Malcolm and the possibility of a trial. He just leapt into the air and burst into tears. 'That's what I want, Mum,' he sobbed. 'That's what I want.'

I was just as bad when she told me. I couldn't believe it was true. It was the most daunting thing I've ever felt – that Manchester United had been watching my son. All I ever wanted was for him to play football – I hoped he would make it as a pro but never in my wildest dreams did I ever think he would be good enough for United.

Malcolm didn't ring that night – he came round to the house instead. He sat in our front room and spoke to me, Sandra and David.

'I think your son has everything we're looking for,' he said. 'He's got talent, he's got discipline and I really think he can make it. Don't worry about him being a bit on the small side – you're big, your family is big. He'll be a big lad.

'We'd like him to come up for trials and go through the system. I'll pick him up, he'll be looked after perfectly and he'll want for nothing.'

I remember looking over at David and saying, 'Well, mate, what do you want to do?'

He could hardly speak. I don't think he'd ever thought his dream would become a reality but here it was on a plate.

We had always kept David informed about his career. Whenever we got a letter or a phone call from a club, we told him. It was his life and we always thought he had a right to be involved in the decisions. We were there to guide him – we'd tell him what we thought but, at the end of the day, it was up to him. We would never have made him do something he didn't want to do.

It wasn't long after that Sandra got the shock of her life. It was a Friday night and when I got home from work, she just said: 'You'll never believe what's just happened. I've had a phone call … a phone call from Alex Ferguson.'

I could hardly take in what she'd said. Ferguson? Ringing our home? To speak to us? It couldn't be true. But it was.

'Well, what did he say?' I asked.

'I didn't hear half of what he said. He's got such a strong Scottish accent I couldn't understand it. All I got was him saying: "You've got a highly talented son. I'm just phoning to see if everything is all right and to let you know he'll be fine with us."'

Just a few weeks later – on 25 October 1987 – United were playing a Sunday game at West Ham and Malcolm rang up and asked if we'd like to go to the game.

Just as the phone call was ending, he said, 'Oh, by the way, the boss was wondering if you'd like to have a meal with him the night before in the team hotel.'

Again, we could hardly believe it. It seemed impossible that we would be sitting down for a meal with Alex Ferguson.

I'd never even spoken to Alex before and the only contact with us had been that one phone call to Sandra. As the week went by, we got more and more nervous. We were desperate to impress him because we knew he thought so much of David and didn't want to do anything that might spoil that.

On the Saturday night, Malcolm picked us up and drove us over to the team hotel in his brown Ford Sierra. We were ushered into the team room and were stunned to see all the players there ready to begin their meal. We were shown to the top table, where Alex Ferguson was sitting with Bobby Charlton, some of the directors and a few of the coaches.

It was the most daunting thing I've ever done – sitting there with the most senior people at United and the player I had idolized all my life. And all that I could think about was that they were interested in my son. It was incredible.

Ferguson was brilliant, chatting away to me and Sandra, although I can't remember anything of what he said. He treated David perfectly, telling him to get up and talk to the first-team players and get their autographs. They were great with him too, having a laugh and a joke with him. They were all there – Bryan Robson, Steve Bruce, Peter Schmeichel, Gary Pallister – ruffling his hair and sharing a bit of banter.

As the meal was finishing, the conversation turned towards the next day's game. United were favourites of course, even though they were away, and everyone seemed confident of winning. Then out of the blue, Ferguson suddenly asked: 'Has David got a United tracksuit?'

Well, David had got just about every United tracksuit that had come out since he'd been born, so that was no problem.

'Yes,' I said. 'We've just got him the new one.'

'Right, he'll be our mascot on Sunday then,' said Ferguson.

That was it, no argument.

When I think back now I can see how Ferguson was doing everything he could to impress us and David. He wanted to make a good impression, even though he knew both David and I were United nuts.

At the time, we were too nervous to really think about why Ferguson was doing all this but now, of course, I can see he was desperate to get David on the books to stop him going to another club. What he didn't realize was that we were so desperate for him to play for United that we'd have turned down any other club.

We hardly slept that night. We were so excited at the prospect of David joining up with the team again and meeting Ferguson and all the other people at United.

Malcom picked us up again on the Sunday morning and we arrived at the ground in plenty of time. As we got to Upton Park, the United team coach pulled up and Ferguson spotted us as soon as he got off.

'You all ready, then?' he said to David, who nodded sheepishly and followed the manager into the ground.

We got taken up to the directors' lounge, where we were met by a friend of Alex Ferguson's, Joe Glanville, who is president of the Manchester United supporters' association in Malta. We got chatting to him and then suddenly he said, 'Look down there, on the pitch. Your boy's having a warm-up.'

Sandra and I turned to look out of the window and there was David having a kickabout with all the first-team players on the Upton Park pitch. I couldn't believe it – my son kicking around with the likes of Bryan Robson and Gordon Strachan. It was just an amazing sight.

Of course, David got his picture taken as the mascot and then trotted off the pitch. I suppose we thought he'd come up and join us to watch the game but the next time we saw him, he was sitting on the bench beside Ferguson. And that's where he spent the whole game, which ended in a 1–1 draw.

Ferguson was brilliant with David and kept talking to him through the game. We asked David what he'd said later, but he wouldn't tell us.

'Mr Ferguson told me not to repeat anything he'd said,' was his only answer.

When we got home that night we couldn't wait for *Match of the Day*. There, on the bench next to Ferguson, was our son David. It was brilliant – and it was a turning point.

At the time, David was still training at Spurs once a week but then he started going up for training in the school holidays with United. He would go up for a week at a time and stay in dormitories with boys from all over the country and from Ireland. Keith Gillespie and Robbie Savage, who have both made good professional careers, were there at the same time.

There'd be about 20 or 30 of them there at any one time, so I'm sure it was a bit nerve-wracking for David at first but we never had to push him to go. In the summer holidays, he'd spend six weeks on the bounce up there – I'm not sure many other boys were allowed to do that but David always seemed to be treated a bit better than the rest.

On those training weeks, Malcolm Fidgeon used to call for him at home at 8am sharp on the Monday morning to take him up.

David would always be up extra early on those days. He'd be in his Man United tracksuit and be checking out the window every five minutes to see if Malcolm was there. And David would keep nipping to the toilet, so we knew he was nervous.

All of a sudden, he'd see Malcolm: 'He's here, he's here.' One last trip to the toilet and he'd be off. He'd wave as the car left but I don't remember any tears or anything like that. We were all a bit sad to see him go, but we knew it was what he really wanted to do. And David wanted to do it so badly, he was happy to sacrifice a few home comforts to get it.

It was hard for me and his mum when he went away for those weeks. He was so young and even though we knew he was desperate to be a United player, it was a long way to go. We knew United would look after him – and they always did superbly – but there was always a nagging little doubt.

David used to ring us every night and we never really felt he was too homesick. He just talked about the football the whole time and we gave him all the love and support we could.

Other professional clubs were still sniffing around us and we were keen to keep the door open, just in case United didn't work out. We had several approaches from Arsenal and Spurs. In fact, we used to go to watch matches at Spurs quite a lot because they gave us free tickets.

We got one letter from Everton, asking what his situation was, and another from Nottingham Forest offering David a trial. Obviously, Forest had a fantastic reputation for developing young talent so I said to David, 'Forest sounds all right, I reckon you should go up there and have a week's training with them.'

'OK, Dad,' he said, 'yeah, sounds good.'

He went upstairs to his room and all of a sudden he shouted down from his room, 'Dad, when do Forest want me to go up?'

I told him the date.

'I'M NOT GOING!'

'What do you mean, you're not going?'

'That's my Man United training week and I'm not going to miss that. I'm not going to Forest.'

United were brilliant about keeping in touch with us and making sure David was progressing well. Whenever they were playing in London, we would get tickets and David and I would go along. Of course, it was fantastic for me as a fan of the club and it was wonderful to see David's love for the club grow.

But David was still training with Tottenham, although they didn't seem to be trying quite as hard to impress him, or us. While Fergie seemed to know all about David and us as a family, the then manager of Spurs, David Pleat, didn't seem quite as clued up.

I remember one day at Spurs, David was just walking off the pitch with the youth coach John Moncur when they saw Pleat. He wandered over and John introduced him to David.

'Mr Pleat, this is one of the young lads we're hoping to sign.'

Pleat ruffled David's hair and just said, 'Oh, you'll have to grow a bit more first.' That was a bit of a kick in the teeth for a young lad who was just starting out.

Despite that, Spurs were the first pro club to make David a concrete offer. He had done well there and was popular with the coaches. He was just coming up to his 14th birthday, the earliest you could sign schoolboy forms, when Moncur made his first move.

He invited us to White Hart Lane in January 1989 for a friendly Spurs were playing against Monaco and wanted to take us out for dinner first. We had a pretty good idea of what he wanted to talk about and he quickly made it clear Spurs wanted David. He said they'd just taken on another couple of young lads but promised

David would get a better deal than either of them. Over dinner, John said the manager, Terry Venables, who'd come back from Barcelona by this time, wanted to meet us all.

When we arrived at the ground, we were taken up to Venables's office. We knocked on the door and went in. As we walked through the door, Venables was scrabbling around on the floor looking for some pins or something he'd knocked off his desk.

He just said, 'Oh, sorry – I'll be with you in a minute.' Eventually, he got back in his chair and then threw his arms behind his head and plonked his feet on the table.

Then he said, 'Well, John, what have you got to tell me about the lad?'

John replied: 'He's got everything this club wants and he's a brilliant little player. I'd love to sign him.'

Then Terry turned to David and said, 'Well, Dave, do you like it here?'

'Yes, Mr Venables.'

'Do you like the coaching here?'

'Yes, Mr Venables.'

'Do you get on with the coaches?'

'Yes, thanks. They're great.'

'Would you like to sign for us?'

Well, that was the big question. There it was, the chance to sign for a professional club and start making a career in the game.

David was as cool as anything, though. He thought for a moment and then just said, 'Can I think about it?'

'Yes, no problem. Just come back when you're ready,' said Venables.

I was so proud of David. It was a huge thing for a 13-year-old to ask for time to think about things. But I suppose that just shows how much confidence he had. On the way out, John really started going to work on us, telling us how much the club believed in David and how they would really look after him.

I told him the final decision had to rest with David. We went on to watch the game but it didn't turn out too well for Spurs – they lost 3–1.

But on the way home, David started talking about things.

'Did you see that, Dad? The way Terry Venables sat in his chair and put his feet up on the desk? And when he asked me if I wanted to sign, I wanted to say to him, "No, I want to go to Man United." But I thought I'd better not do that. It was good there, Dad, but I really want United.'

Of course, at that stage United hadn't even made an offer but it was another example of the confidence he had in his own ability.

He still had a few more training sessions to finish at Spurs before he turned 14, when he would have to decide. On what turned out to be his very last training night at Spurs, they arranged a game. And David played out of his skin – as good as I can ever remember. He was shooting, chipping, stopping the ball and his work rate was incredible. It was as if he was saying: 'Look, this is what you're going to miss out on.' I don't think that was a conscious thought but it was very much the impression he gave.

He came off the pitch and said, 'Dad, I really enjoyed that, it was fantastic. Shame it's the last one.'

I was watching the game and, as always, I'd been standing on my own. I liked to make my own judgement and if I wanted to say something I didn't want to feel I had to watch my words. But this particular night, I could feel John Moncur's eyes boring into me. I knew he wanted to talk to me and at the end of the game he came over.

'I'll come straight to the point,' he said. 'I know David's going up to Manchester in a couple of weeks but will you do me a favour? Will you let me know what they offer? We'll give him anything to join us. A six-year contract, a signing-on fee, whatever you want. But please let me know what they offer.'

As David and I drove home, I told him about the offer – the

six-year contract and that they'd take care of all his clothes and boots and that they'd offer him a signing-on fee of about £70,000 or £80,000.

He sat back and went quiet for a moment. Then he said, 'Cor, that's not bad, is it? When I'm 18, I can get a Porsche!'

Three weeks later, we were up in Manchester to meet Alex Ferguson and hear what they had to offer David. We'd already talked about it and agreed he would go there if they could match the six-year deal Spurs were offering – two as a schoolboy, two as a youth trainee and two as a professional.

That six-year deal was the most important thing for me. It was guaranteed work and the money was nowhere near as vital as the length of contract.

Our meeting with Ferguson took place on David's 14th birthday, 2 May 1989, when United had a home game against Wimbledon in the old First Division.

David, Sandra and I were driven up to Old Trafford by Malcolm, who was desperate for United to sign David, and his wife Joan. It was a huge thing for Malcolm, to get a young lad from the London area into United, and he'd invested so much time and effort in David. I think he was as excited as we were on the long drive.

We stopped at a service station on the way up and David and I wandered off to stretch our legs.

I put my arm around him and said, 'Do you know how proud I am? We're going up to Manchester so you can talk to United. It's my dream, it's your dream. But the only thing I'll say, David, is that if they don't offer you the six years, you should go to Tottenham.'

'Oh, no, Dad,' he said, 'I really want to go to United.'

'Dave, listen,' I replied. 'You've got six years. The money side of it doesn't interest me at all, that will come in time. The most important thing is getting a long contract to see you through.'

He wasn't happy to hear that – I think he'd have said yes to United if they'd offered a one-month contract and £5 a week.

When we arrived at Old Trafford, Ferguson interrupted his lunch to come down and meet us. He organized some lunch for us at the ground and said he'd see us after the game. We went back to the hotel to get showered and changed and then headed back to Old Trafford.

As we drove there, I remembered seeing a programme on television years earlier about George Best signing for United and seeing his parents at the time. They'd looked so proud, if a little nervous about what the future might hold. I'd often dreamed of my son doing the same thing but now that it was about to happen, I could hardly believe it. It was the most amazing feeling.

Joe Brown, the youth development manager, showed us up to the manager's office. As the door swung open, it felt like we were walking into the biggest room in the world. We were completely overwhelmed by it all. There was just this big desk in the middle of the room, but it seemed massive.

We shook hands and Ferguson started having a laugh and a joke with David, who was sporting a new spiky haircut. 'Oh, you're getting taller every day,' said Fergie. 'And I don't think much of the new hairstyle.'

We sat down and the manager came straight to the point: 'Well, we all know why you've come up here. David has everything it takes to become a Man United player; he has everything it takes to become a Man United legend.

'We've kept a dossier on him for the last couple of years and everything in it shows he is an incredible player who we believe will get better and better. He's a credit to his mum and dad, he's a polite lad, he works hard and has everything we're looking for. We want him to become a Man United player.'

I just sat there stunned. I didn't know what to say. Alex Ferguson was telling us he wanted David to join the club I'd supported all my life and I was struck dumb.

Then Ferguson said: 'We can offer David two, two and two.'

I didn't understand what he meant. Two, two and two? What the bloody hell did that mean? But I looked over at David and first he started smiling, then he broke into a laugh. Of course, he'd twigged quicker than me that Ferguson was offering us exactly what we wanted: a six-year deal – two years as a schoolboy, the next two years on their youth training scheme as an apprentice and the next two years as a full-time professional.

'What do you want to do, David?' I said.

'I want to sign it,' he replied. No ifs, buts or anything. He just signed there and then and that was it. My dreams – and his – had come true.

We called Malcolm in and had a couple of photos done. He shook our hands and then took David out to meet the first-team squad, who were having a meal before the game. The first player they saw was Bryan Robson, who had already met David.

Ferguson walked over to his captain and said, 'Bryan, I just wanted to let you know that David has just signed for the club.'

Bryan stood up, shook David's hand and said, 'Well done, you couldn't have joined a better club.'

We stayed in Manchester that night and had a fantastic meal at Old Trafford, complete with a specially prepared birthday cake for David, before watching United beat Wimbledon 1–0. We were given a tour of the ground the next day but it all passed in a blur. It was as though I was in a trance – I couldn't really take in what had happened.

My son had signed for the club I'd supported all my life and had a chance to join the list of legends I'd always idolized. I just put my arms around him and gave him a huge hug.

FROM SCHOOLBOY TO FIRST TEAM 1989-1995

'Our lives changed for ever on the day David signed for Manchester United. From that moment, our family's whole future was wrapped up in that club.'

Sandra and I went up to Manchester every time David played – and I mean every time. I think we only missed three or four games of his entire United career, starting with B team games and progressing through the A team, the reserves and eventually the first team. It was 200 miles door to door and I shudder to think how far we've travelled to follow our son's football career.

Of course, for the first year and a half of his contract he was only allowed to go up during the school holidays. But everyone realized his future was only going in one direction so after he turned 15, he was allowed to take the odd week off school to be at United.

He used to spend all the holidays up there – a couple of weeks at Christmas and Easter, plus four or five in the summer. He never had a moment's hesitation in going and never seemed to be worried about it. Even though he hardly knew anyone at first and was staying in a large dormitory with boys from all over the country, he was desperate to go.

The whole family was thrilled for him. They all knew how much it meant to him and even though we were all aware of the failure rate among young professional footballers this was the chance for David to live his dream, for however long it lasted. Even his Tottenham-mad granddad was pleased for him.

It was clear even then that United thought David was something special. He was treated so well and was allowed to wander just about anywhere at Old Trafford to get autographs, even before he'd signed. I knew it was a ploy to secure him but it never seemed as calculating as that.

There was one brilliant time when we went to see United play Liverpool in the 1990 Charity Shield at Wembley. David was due to go up to Manchester the next week for training, so we asked if he could travel back with the team on the coach after the game.

I think it was all organized by Nobby Stiles, one of the youth coaches who'd worked with David, and Joe Brown, the youth development officer. Nobby was also a United legend, having won the World Cup with England in 1966 and the European Cup with United a couple of years later.

After the Charity Shield, which ended 1-1, we were taken down to the coach entrance at Wembley, underneath the old twin towers. We waited there until the team bus appeared, with Nobby sitting in one of the front seats. It drew up alongside us, the automatic door swung open and David jumped aboard. I don't think he even looked back at us.

The doors closed and the coach moved off, leaving us waving at the blacked-out windows as it started the journey north.

Of course, as soon as David got up there I was on the phone to him. 'Who did you sit next to? What did they say to you? What was it like?'

I think I was almost more thrilled than David because he'd been with a lot of the players who were my heroes. I'd supported United all my life and to see your son get on the coach with the first team … well, words can hardly describe it. I've always been a little starstruck, so to see my son mixing with players I idolized was incredible.

But David wasn't anything like as excited as I was. 'Oh, I just sat up the back,' he said. 'The players all spoke to me but I didn't really say much. They gave me a drink so I was fine.'

I was so proud of him. He seemed to take it all in his stride but I couldn't stop thinking about it, or telling people about it.

That was typical of the way United treated David. Alex Ferguson took him under his wing and gave him little perks and privileges that other lads weren't given.

Nobby was a big influence on David's early career at United. Even though David and the other boys were far too young to remember Nobby's glory days, United made sure they knew exactly what he'd done for the club.

Nobby was a hard man as a player and just as hard as a coach. He wouldn't let his lads get away with anything – but he would always stand up for them. And that was never more obvious than in a game David played at Littleton Road, United's second training ground, not long after he'd joined them.

The United kids were up against a team of Irish lads, who were going in really hard on every tackle. It got pretty rough and the studs were flying.

We were standing on the touchline and suddenly this big lad went in really hard on David and kicked him up in the air. Well, Nobby did his nut. He marched on to the pitch and started yelling: 'Oi, big feller, come and f***ing try it with me, you bastard. You think you're so f***ing hard, well let's see how f***ing hard you are against me … Come on, come and f***ing try it.'

Eventually, the ref managed to calm the situation down and David got to his feet. You could see Nobby was still seething but as he turned to walk off the pitch he caught my eye. He looked all embarrassed and said: 'Oh, I'm sorry, Mr Beckham. Sorry about the language. I didn't realize you were there. Sorry.'

'Don't worry,' I said. 'I was thinking just the same!'

Whenever David was up in Manchester we would speak every day on the phone. Often, he'd tell me how he'd been training with the first team, working alongside some of the biggest names in the game – Bryan Robson, Steve Bruce, Gary Pallister, Mark Hughes.

That was a hallmark of Alex Ferguson's management. He involved the boys and gave them the chance to play alongside their heroes. One of the great things at United was that all the players – from the young lads to the first-teamers – trained on pitches next door to each other. So the kids were almost in touching distance of the superstars and could see how hard they worked. I think that was great for them and helped encourage them to work just as hard.

Fergie was brilliant with all the boys. He knew all their names, right from day one, and seemed to know everything about them. I would say that was the main difference between him and other managers.

I remember once going up to the training ground when David was already in the first team and seeing Fergie with a group of about six lads. Fergie knew every one of them by first name, even though they can't have been more than 12.

One of them had a really dodgy haircut and Fergie was ribbing him: 'You wouldn't get away with that haircut in my first team.' Then he went round every one and gave them little tips – 'you've got to get your passing going' or 'you've got to work on your left foot' or 'you've got to get tackling more in the middle of the park'. So not only did he know them all by name, but he knew the parts of their game which needed work. That was typical of him.

After David signed that first contract, he was playing for five different teams. There were occasional games for United, plus games for his old Ridgeway side, Chingford High School, Waltham Forest district and Essex county. It was a hectic schedule but he never gave it a second thought.

All he ever wanted to do was play football and he was prepared to give up an awful lot to achieve his dream. I can well remember his mates knocking on the door on a Saturday night to try to persuade him to come out but he'd insist on staying in to get an early night because he had a game the next day.

By the time David signed for United, Ridgeway had merged with Brimsdown Rovers, who had their own ground over in Enfield. So many Ridgeway boys had gone on to professional clubs that we were sometimes struggling to put out a decent side, so it made sense. It was quite hard for me, Stuart and Steve to accept the merger but we realized it was in the best interest of the boys and that was always the most important thing.

We ended up running a team at Brimsdown for a couple of seasons – but my one abiding memory of that period is of David being sent off for the first time in his career. It's not something he was very proud of – and I took it even worse.

It came right at the end of his Sunday career in a Cup game for Brimsdown in Enfield. David had been booked early on for a tackle so he was on a bit of a knife-edge from the word go. But he's never been good at playing half-heartedly and that's what cost him.

He clattered into another tackle, thought he'd won the ball fairly but was stunned when the ref blew for a free-kick. He was furious and really thought it was an unfair decision. Instead of keeping it to himself, he gave the ref a right mouthful and ended it by telling him to eff off.

The ref had no choice but to send him off. I suppose David was a bit like me – I can't remember how many times I was sent off for swearing at refs, but it was a fair few.

Of course, I gave David a right good telling-off on the way home but I didn't really go for it all guns blazing. He knew what my record was like so it would have seemed a bit hypocritical.

David was lucky enough to have some brilliant coaches in those early days, who really gave him encouragement to fulfil his dream.

His PE teacher at school was a guy called John Bulloch, who knew how to get the best out of David. The school was better known for rugby when David arrived and hadn't really had much of a football team at all. But David and a few of the other Ridgeway lads soon changed that – and John played a key role in getting it all going.

David kept in touch with him long after he went to United and used to write to him and send him photos. John died a few years ago now but he deserves a lot of credit for helping make David the player he is now.

David's coach at Waltham Forest was Don Wilshire, who recognized David's talent immediately. In all honesty, he was a bit too soft sometimes, especially if the boys were mucking around a bit. Don didn't have it in him to really have a go at them and the boys knew that, but he definitely had their best interests at heart.

Martin Heather coached the Essex county side and he had a huge knowledge of football. He used to work for Wimbledon and gave all the lads a really good grounding. He was never afraid to try new ideas and even took David's Under-15 side on a trip to Dallas.

I remember one game David played for Essex on 20 October 1990 when he came up against a certain Robbie Fowler at Anfield. Robbie was playing for Merseyside and helped his side to a 3–2 win. There were some great players on show that day, including Dele Adebola and Anthony Grant for Merseyside, and Ryan Kirby, Jason Brissett and Mark Hoddle for Essex.

That first 18 months at Old Trafford really flew by and it wasn't long before David was making plans to move up to Manchester full-time. His two years as a schoolboy were almost up and he was

THE E.S.F.A. / adidas UNDER 16
INTER COUNTY COMPETITION FINAL

MERSEYSIDE C.S.F.A.			ESSEX C.S.F.A.	
(ALL RED)			(WHITE SHORTS & BLACK SHIRTS)	
GK	JOHN CARRIDGE	Sefton	GK	STEVEN REEVES	Barking & Dagenham
2	STUART JONES	Sefton	2	JOEL SWAIN	Harlow & W. Essex
3	MARK STALKER	Sefton	3	MARK WARREN	Barking & Dagenham
4	ASHLEY NEAL	Sefton	4	LEE FOWLER	Barking & Dagenham
5	PAUL BROWN	Liverpool	5	GAVIN SHARPE	Thurrock
6	ANTHONY GRANT (C)	Liverpool	6	SCOTT CANHAM	Newham
7	CHRIS RIMMER	Sefton	7	DAVID BECKHAM	Waltham Forest
8	EDDIE McCULLAGH	Liverpool	8	RYAN KIRBY	Waltham Forest
9	ROBERT FOWLER	Liverpool	9	NANA BOACHIE	Waltham Forest
10	JONATHON CROSS	Wirral	10	PETER LINGLEY	Redbridge
11	DELE ADEBOLA	Liverpool	11	JASON BRISSETT	Waltham Forest
Subs:			Subs:	
	ALAN BARKER	St. Helens		ALAN SPRING	Colchester & NE Essex
	CARL CONROY	Liverpool		JAMIE DEAR	Redbridge
	KIERON ENGLAND	Sefton		MATT HOLMAN	Harlow & West Essex
	PETER GICK	Liverpool		ROGER GELL	Thurrock
	DAVID GRINDLEY	St. Helens		MARK HODDLE	Harlow & West Essex
	TERRY JONES	Kirkby / Knowsley		PAUL FLOWERS	Waltham Forest
	STEVE LANE	Sefton		JAY BIGWOOD	Redbridge
	ALAN MALKESON	Sefton		CHRISTIAN DAVIES	Colchester & NE Essex
	SCOTT WHITE	St. Helens			

Team Manager: Mr Ken Davies
Asst. Managers: Mr Mike Dickinson & Mr Bob Lynch

Team Manager: Mr Martyn Heather
Asst. Manager: Mr Pat Walker

REFEREE: Mr A M Beddoes (Shropshire CFA) LINESMEN: Mr A W Davies (Shropshire CFA) & Mr P Lea (Lancashire CFA)
RESERVE OFFICIAL: Mr R Westwood (Liverpool CFA) BALL BOYS: Under 12's Gateacre Community School

The duration of the game is 80 minutes each way. If scores are level at the end of 80 mins, the trophy will be shared. Each team may use a maximum of two substitutes during the game.

The match programme from the Merseyside v Essex under-16 inter-county
competition final in which David played against the young Robbie Fowler.

about to become a proper YTS apprentice. He was 15 and a half
and about to leave home permanently. That was a huge step for
him – and just as huge for me.

I have to admit I was devastated when he left home. We were
mates, we were friends, we played football together, we socialized
together, we did everything together. It was so tough. It left a big
hole in my life.

It was tough for me personally and for Sandra. Our only consolation was that he was going to the one place in the world he
wanted to be. We were lucky in that we could afford to go up
every week and watch him play football.

But the house really seemed empty without him. It's funny how
much difference one person can make to a household. Suddenly,
I was the only male in the house and with my daughters growing

up fast I really felt it.

Once David was full-time at United his football dominated our lives completely. But it was never a chore – it was just the way Sandra and I enjoyed ourselves. We weren't a boozy couple and we never really went to the pictures or the theatre – football, and David's football in particular, was everything to us. It became the whole focus of our lives and we used to look forward to going up to Manchester at weekends.

I can't say it was easy. When David first went there, we had no idea where any of the grounds were. To be honest, the only time I'd heard of places like Rochdale or Blackpool was when the football results were being read out on Saturday afternoons.

On match days, we'd try to leave the house by 5am to make sure we could arrive at United's training ground, The Cliff, by 9am. That was when the team bus would set off for away games. We used to follow the coach to the ground to be there in plenty of time for the 11am kick-off. It might sound crazy to some people but we loved every minute of it.

If there's one regret I have it's that perhaps my two daughters felt a little pushed out by the amount of time we devoted to David.

Lynne was that much older than David so when we started going up to Manchester every weekend, she usually chose to stay behind with friends or at home. Joanne was so much younger that she wasn't given any choice – she was just bundled in the back of the car and taken with us. Not that she really minded, because she came to love football. She idolized her brother then and still does today.

Lynne is married to Colin and they have two children, Georgina, who is about a year older than David's first son, Brooklyn, and Freddie, who was born in 2002 and is already showing some football promise. Lynne is expecting her third child and is happy to live her life her own way out of the limelight. She doesn't like all the rubbish that goes with being David's sister but she loves her brother.

Joanne and David aren't as close now as when they were kids, but that's part of growing up. David is married and living in Spain, so obviously they can't see as much of each other as they used to. But they still talk on the phone and she knows a lot of the people David knows.

I think the girls accepted the situation when they were kids, although they didn't always like it. They used to accuse us of spoiling David and, to a certain extent, I think they were right. But I'm as proud now of the way the girls have handled everything that has come with being David's sister as I am of him.

Sometimes, Sandra, Joanne and I would go up to Manchester twice a week to watch games and I'm sure that really helped David settle in. He knew we were there for him. We used to take biscuits with us whenever we went and we made sure he had everything he wanted in his digs – a stereo, a television and a radio. And I'd always slip him a few quid because he was only earning £29.50 a week at United and that didn't go far.

United always made sure their youngsters were put up with local families. They kept a list of all the suitable homes and helped David choose somewhere they thought would be good for him.

The first place David went to was beautiful – a large, semi-detached house in Bury New Road, very close to The Cliff, in Salford. Unfortunately, David had a bit of an upset with them because the dad gave him a clip round the ear for getting home late and forgetting his key. David had to ring the doorbell and the dad wasn't too pleased.

David called us up to tell us what had happened and I was furious, as were United. I got straight on to the dad to tell him to keep his hands to himself and to leave my son alone.

The club moved David straight away to another place on Lower Broughton Road. Again, it was a very nice place, where David shared a room with another Old Trafford apprentice called John O'Kane, whom he knew from his summer trips up to United. David was a very tidy boy and liked all his things in order. But the landlady used to go into their room and move things around, which he hated.

We told the club and they moved him again – this time to Annie and Tommy Kay's home, a lovely place almost directly opposite The Cliff. It was a large, end-of-terrace house on a corner plot and the Kays were a fantastic couple. Their children had left home so they had plenty of room for the United boys.

Annie really loved David and both Sandra and I got on very well with her and Tommy. David ended up staying there until he signed his first pro contract, when he could afford to buy a place of his own.

One of the main reasons he liked it so much was because Annie gave him the room that Mark Hughes, the old United striker and now Blackburn manager, had once used. Hughes had been one of David's boyhood heroes so he was really chuffed about that.

On a typical match day in those first few years, we'd take David back to his digs after the game and wait while he got changed. Then we'd take him out shopping and go for a meal or go to watch United if they were at home and then go out for dinner. Of course, that often meant we weren't leaving Manchester until 8pm or later so it was a heck of a long day.

That was pretty much every weekend and I can honestly say I never remember any tears on his part when it was time for us to go. He was so single-minded about what he wanted to do.

He sacrificed everything for football. At an age where most boys are starting to go out on their own, discovering girls and drink and learning how to have a good time, he was devoting himself completely to football. I'm not saying he lived like a monk but he gave up a lot of his teenage life to football and very few lads were prepared to do that. He rarely went out and, if he did, he made sure he was always home by 10pm.

His first girlfriend was Deana, who was from Manchester. She was petite and very good-looking and I think he went out with her for about three years. Sandra and I met her parents and David got quite close to her dad, who was a Liverpool season ticket-holder. David and her dad would sometimes go out for a drink together and I know David remembers those days very fondly.

I think his only other vice, if you can call it that, was snooker. He and a few of the other United lads used to sometimes go and play in a local snooker hall but David was always very sensible about his social life. He used to knock around with his team-mates, like Gary and Phil Neville, Nicky Butt and Paul Scholes, but he knew you couldn't burn the candle at both ends if you wanted to be a professional footballer.

I'd always drummed into him how important it was to keep his feet on the ground. Time after time I'd say, 'David, just because you're at Manchester United and you've signed a long contract it doesn't mean you've made it. You've got to try hard every day and keep improving. You've got to take the next step. Don't be a Billy Big-Head. Only when you're holding down a regular place in the first team can you say, "I've arrived." '

David accepted all that completely and knew what he had to do. He always went in for extra training and worked as hard as he could. In a way, I'm more proud of the way he knuckled down during those first couple of years in Manchester than of anything else.

I can't pretend it was always easy. His family were obviously a long way away and I know he felt lonely at times.

I remember ringing up one day and he said: 'I had a nightmare today, Dad. I couldn't get anything right. None of the passes were working, my tackling was bad. I just couldn't get it.'

We longed to put an arm round him and reassure him but we had to do the best we could from 200 miles away. We just had to say: 'Don't worry, everyone has bad days at work and you're no different. You'll be better tomorrow.'

We'd sometimes offer to come up, especially if he sounded a bit down, but he always told us not to bother. And it would blow over and never really cause a problem.

Ferguson's management was spot-on with the young lads. Some days he'd get one or two of them over and say: 'Come on, you can train with the first team today.' He didn't make a big deal out of it but you can imagine what effect that had on a young boy just starting out. That happened a fair few times to David and he'd be out there with Mark Hughes, Gary Pallister, Steve Bruce, Peter Schmeichel and the others – the phone calls on those days were always very happy.

I know he did the right thing by going to United. If he'd gone anywhere else, he might have ended up as a player but I doubt he'd have been as successful. In a way, living away from home at such an early age helped toughen him up and make him even more determined to succeed. If he'd gone to Spurs, say, and stayed living at home I'm not certain he would have been as successful as he is. He fulfilled his potential by going to United. He was playing with the best players in the business and they grew together.

He didn't have a lot of time to mope at United. They were training quite hard, often both morning and afternoon, and it was pretty tough. But he had a good support network there. Besides the Kays and Fergie, he also had Joe Brown, United's youth development officer, and his wife Connie, who were the loveliest people you could wish to meet.

They'd been close to David from the first time he went up to Old Trafford and Connie took a particular shine to him. She always used to say: 'He's one of those boys you could really give a hug and cuddle to.' And she really loved his spiky hair.

It was thrilling seeing him develop in those first few years at United. He was getting taller, bigger and more powerful. His outlook improved a lot in those first couple of years at United. He got more confident in his own ability and in the way he related to other people. Obviously, his football improved and he was really enjoying life.

He was playing alongside better and better players, yet coping with everything they threw at him. In fact, he did more than cope – he shone. And nothing could make his father prouder than that.

He was starting to play in front of some pretty decent crowds, as well. Even the junior sides at United used to get two or three thousand for home games on Saturday mornings – and very often the first-team players or Fergie would be there as well. Bryan Robson used to turn up at a lot of games and sometimes you'd see Fergie watching from the first-floor window of the changing rooms. There were many times when he'd do more than watch – he'd bang on the window and start shouting down to the boys.

The other person who took a real interest in David was Eric Harrison, who was then reserve team coach at Old Trafford. That might have been his title but he took a close interest in all the teams leading up to the reserves as well, so he soon got to know David.

He was a magnificent coach simply because he knew how to treat the boys properly. He had what seemed like a sixth sense so that he knew when to encourage them, when to cuddle them and when to have a go at them. He was like a magician with boys and worth probably ten times what United paid him.

After all, he brought through players like David, the Nevilles, Nicky Butt, Paul Scholes, Ryan Giggs, Robbie Savage, Keith Gillespie and Mark Hughes. You can hardly begin to work out how much that lot is worth.

The boys really respected him. He used to swear, shout, scream and holler at them, often using some of the choicest words you'll ever hear, but somehow he managed to do it in a way that wasn't offensive.

He liked to watch games from the canteen, on the first floor above the dressing rooms, and if he saw something he didn't like,

the MANCHESTER UNITED FOOTBALL CLUB plc OLD TRAFFORD MANCHESTER M16 0RA
Registered Office: Old Trafford, Manchester, M16 0RA

Registered No. 95489 England
Telephone:
061-872 1661 (Office)
061-872 0199 (Ticket and Match Enquiries)
061-872 3488 (Commercial Department)
Fax No: 061-873 7210
Telex: 666564 United G

Chief Executive	Manager	Secretary	Commercial Manager
C. Martin Edwards	Alex Ferguson	Kenneth R. Merrett	D. A. McGregor

Rev. Roger Sutton (Chaplin)

RS/LL

2 July 1991

Mr & Mrs Beckham

Dear Mr and Mrs Beckham

We are very much looking forward to David joining the Club. We hope his time with us will be very enjoyable and that he will be able to settle into the club quickly.

My role as Chaplin of the Club is to try and provide care for all its employees. To be a confidential listening ear to any person facing any personal difficulties and then to assist in any way I can.

So if I can help in any way over the course of the next two years, please do not hesitate to contact me. If you are worried or concerned about any aspect of David's time with us please just ring me or write to me at my home address given above.

This is obviously an invitation to David also. I shall try and meet him as soon as possible after he arrives.

I'm looking forward to meeting your son and hopefully yourselves at a later date.

Yours faithfully

President: Sir Matt Busby CBE.
Directors: C.M. Edwards (Chairman), J.M. Edelson, R. Charlton CBE, E.M. Watkins, A.M. A Midani, N. Burrows, R.L. Olive, M. Knighton.

This letter from the Chaplain at United demonstrates how welcome the people at Manchester United made David, as well as Sandra and me.

he'd throw open the window and start screaming and shouting.

'Oi, you stupid little bastard, stop trying to f***ing well hit those f***ing Hollywood passes!'

And David knew that was aimed at him, because he was always trying to hit a 50-yard pass rather than a simple five-yard one.

There was one game, though, when not even Eric could have complained about David. It was at Littleton Road, when David was about 16 and playing for the A team against Everton.

It was 1–1 and there wasn't long to go. David picked the ball up just inside his own half and, almost unbelievably, chipped the keeper from there to make it 2–1. Of course, he became instantly famous for doing the very same thing in a League game a few years later, but this was just as incredible. I was standing on the touchline and all around I could hear people saying: 'What a fantastic goal – did he really hit that from inside his own half?' 'What a goal! How the hell did he do that?' It was a great feeling for a father.

I always stood quietly on the side of the pitch whenever I watched David. I was well aware the coaches knew a lot more about football than I did.

But I used to get into David after games to try and help him improve. I wanted him to talk more, to be more like Chris Casper, whose career was ended by a bad injury, or Gary Neville, who were both great talkers on the pitch. That wasn't really David's style, but I knew it was an area he had to work on to realize his potential fully. I think my talking about Cas used to get on David's nerves – which was sort of what I wanted. I always felt he played better with a bit of anger inside him.

Nicky Butt was another player I used as a yardstick for David. He was such a strong lad and he really used to get stuck in. I knew David wasn't that sort of player but I also knew how good it would be if he could add just a little of that strength to his game. Whenever I compared him to Nicky, I could see David bristle but

I knew he'd try that much harder and do that much better in the next game.

Sandra and I were up there so often that we started to make friends with several of the other parents, especially Frank Casper, who used to play for Burnley, and his wife, and the Neville family. Gary and Phil's dad, Neville Neville, has since become a really good friend and we've travelled all over the world watching our sons play for United.

We were treated really well by United. Whenever we went up to watch David we were given seats in the directors' box for the first-team game and the same at away games. And Ferguson always went out of his way to talk to us.

I remember one day we were standing in a lounge at Old Trafford talking and suddenly Ferguson walked in. He spotted us straight away.

'Hello, Mr and Mrs Beckham. How are you?'

'Fine, thanks,' said Sandra.

We started chatting about David's football when suddenly Sandra noticed a famous face on the other side of the room. I think it was Michael Ball, who was playing the lead role in the West End musical *Aspects of Love*. She couldn't resist saying something and Ferguson could see she was a bit starstruck.

'Have you seen the show?' he asked.

'No,' replied Sandra. 'We can't get tickets. It's sold out.'

'Leave it with me.'

We didn't think any more of it until the following Sunday, when the phone went at 8am. We were still in bed but we shot up, thinking it must be bad news.

Instead, it was Fergie. 'I've got you two tickets for the show on Friday night. You just pick them up from the ticket office when you go.'

Another time we were at Tottenham with Sandra's dad Joe, waiting in the lounge for David to come out. Fergie walked in and made a beeline for us. He started taking the mickey a bit because of Joe's passion for Spurs. But as we chatted, in walked the old Norwich manager Ken Brown, who had known Fergie for years.

Fergie spotted him and they started talking about football. But Ferguson made absolutely sure he introduced us to Brown. There was no need to, but that was just the sort of bloke Fergie was and is. He did that every time. He involved us in everything, made us feel part of the club and part of the whole adventure.

One of the best experiences we had in David's early career was going over to Northern Ireland for a tournament called the Milk Cup in 1991. It was an annual competition, in which United fielded a youth side. This year, they had made David captain.

Sandra and I both went over for it – our first 'foreign' trip to watch him – even though we were both a little apprehensive about going to the province.

It was when the Troubles were still on, so the papers and television were full of all the problems and dangers. We were amazed by how many police and soldiers we saw but we still had a wonderful time. The people were very welcoming and seemed really pleased to see us.

We were out there for a week with the United scout, Malcolm Fidgeon, and his wife Joan.

The boys played in several towns across the province and we followed them around. If, for instance, they were playing in Ballymena, we'd spend the day in the town sightseeing and then go to the game in the evening. The boys all stayed together, separate from us, so we didn't have a lot of contact with them, other than at matches.

We spent a couple of nights in a hotel owned by Harry Gregg, the old United goalkeeper who survived the Munich air disaster. He's a real gentleman and made everyone connected with the club feel so welcome. He'd been a hero of mine as a young lad, so it was fantastic to meet him.

Quite a few of the old faces from United were on the trip – Nobby Stiles was the coach and Jimmy Curran, the old physio, was there too. They all looked after us really well and we had a few nights out with them. Jimmy turned out to have a very good singing voice!

I remember once sitting in the hotel where David and the rest of the boys were staying, waiting for him. As he came down the stairs, Jimmy just said: 'All right, there, skipper?'

It was strange to hear my son being spoken to like that. I suppose that was all part of him growing up but my chest puffed out with pride. My son, a captain of a United team!

They played this tournament every year and part of it involved an open-top bus procession through one of the local towns. It was like carnival day and we had to pinch ourselves to believe that our son was involved in something like that. To cap a wonderful week, David's side won the tournament.

David was also part of the team that won United the 1992 Youth Cup after a two-legged final against Crystal Palace – the first time they'd won the trophy for 28 years.

United won the first leg 3–1 and he scored one of the goals, strangely enough with his left foot. It had been raining all afternoon and it was touch and go whether the game would go ahead. The pitch was soaking and a bit boggy but the lads played brilliantly and it was wonderful to see him play a key role in such a big game. We won the second leg at Old Trafford 3–2 to clinch the Cup. The papers next day were full of headlines about Fergie's fledglings, likening the team to the Busby Babes.

Every member of that team was given a pro contract at United and that had never happened before.

David made his first-team debut at the age of just 17 in a Coca-Cola Cup game at Brighton. It was September 1992 and David was still an apprentice but Ferguson obviously never had any doubts about his ability to cope. He often used to use these League Cup games to give younger players a taste of the big time.

David had rung us the night before to tell us he was in the squad for the game but the manager made a point of never announcing the team until an hour before kick-off. He didn't want to give the younger players too much time to get nervous.

David spent the night in the team hotel and then travelled to the Goldstone Ground on the coach with several of his old youth team-mates: Ben Thornley, Gary Neville and Chris Casper. Sandra and I had driven down and we saw them all trot off the coach and into the dressing room. We waited outside, still not sure whether David was playing or not.

All of a sudden, Ben came rushing out, shouting: 'David's on the bench, David's on the bench!' We couldn't believe it but then, a minute or two later, a couple of the other young lads came out and told us the same thing. Even though none of those who came out were playing, they all looked so pleased for David. It was great to see the spirit between them.

It wasn't much of a game but, with about 20 minutes to go, David started running up and down the touchline. We didn't know if he'd just been sent out for a jog, or if he was warming up to come on.

But then he started to take his top off and I shouted to Sandra: 'He's getting changed. Can you believe it? He's coming on!'

If he was anything like as nervous as me it was a wonder he could even move. I was shaking with the tension. This seemed like the fulfilment of everything we'd worked for all those years and I was desperate to see him do well. I was choked – it was all I'd ever dreamed about, seeing my son in a Manchester United shirt.

David came on with 17 minutes to go, as a substitute for Andrei Kanchelskis, and did OK. He made a couple of runs, a few passes and didn't seem out of place, even though United were held to a 1–1 draw.

We waited for him after the game, hoping for a chat before he got on the coach. When he came out, we both gave him a big hug. 'Well done, mate – you did really well.'

'Oh, I was so nervous, Dad. My legs went stiff, I felt sick and I just didn't think I'd be able to do it.'

'Now you know how I felt,' I said.

'But I really enjoyed it. It was incredible. The lads were brilliant to me, talking to me all the time. It was great.'

He was absolutely on cloud nine. I don't think I'd ever seen him happier.

I could hardly speak to Sandra on the journey home. It was well after midnight before we got home but I couldn't get to sleep. I'd recorded the game, so I sat up and just watched those last 17 minutes over and over again.

That was his only look-in for the first team in those early years. He started out playing for United's B team, then moved up to the A team, which is one step below the reserve side.

When he first started at United he was a fair way behind the other lads because he had only been going up in the school holidays. Most of the others came from the Manchester area, so they'd been nursed constantly by United. David had a fair bit to learn tactically, plus he had some growing to do, so it was no surprise he was a slightly late developer.

But United never had any doubts because they gave him his first proper professional contract in 1992. It paid him the princely signing-on fee of £30,000 and put him on wages of £200 a week for the next four years, with various bonus clauses added.

It was a heck of a lot more than the £29.50 he'd been on as a YTS kid – although a long way short of the kind of money he was to make in the future.

It was another two years before David got another chance in the first team – against Galatasaray in a European Cup game in December 1994. He phoned us on the Tuesday and said he thought he might be in the squad because Fergie had said he was going to put a few kids in. United were virtually out of the tournament by then, because earlier results had gone against us.

On the day of the game, we went up to Manchester as usual, hoping against hope he'd be in the side. About an hour before kick-off word filtered up that David was going to start the game – his full debut for United. I could feel the butterflies in my stomach and as kick-off approached I got more and more nervous for him.

This was it – the next rung of the ladder which had started with all those long hours spent at Wadham Lodge, Kelmscott, and at countless pitches in the middle of nowhere watching David play.

Seeing him come out with the team, wearing the red shirt of United in front of a packed Old Trafford was an amazing feeling. I was choked, I was gutted, I was excited, I was thrilled – so many emotions all wrapped up in that moment. The tears welled up in my eyes as he lined up for the pre-match formalities.

He had a fantastic game as well, scoring one goal in front of the Stretford End and making another as United won 4–0. The bloke sitting behind me will never forget that night because when David scored, I leapt up and head-butted him!

David played outstanding football that day – it was as though he was on the right stage at last. The first person to congratulate him on his goal was Eric Cantona, who was already a United legend. It didn't matter that the game was pretty meaningless in terms of the Champions League, with United already out. The important thing was that David had proved he could play football at the very highest level.

When I got home that night, after a 200-mile drive, I was still so excited I couldn't sleep. Lynne had taped the game and I must have watched that goal 30 times. By the weekend, I must have seen it 200 times! My son had scored for Manchester United on his full debut – incredible.

Despite that brilliant night, it was hard to get a grip on how David was doing at United. With two years between first-team appearances, we were a bit worried that things weren't going to work out, although we never let David know we were concerned. And, of course, we had the security of a guaranteed two-year contract as a professional.

We talked to him and he would tell us what he was doing day-to-day but we were never told how he fitted into the manager's thinking. I suppose it's a bit like school – you talk to your children about it, but you never fully understand how well, or how badly, they're doing until you get the exam results.

Our fears grew when David phoned one day early in 1995 and said: 'Here, Dad ... the boss wants me to go out on loan to Preston. What do you think? I don't know whether they rate me ...'

'I think it'll do you good,' I said. 'Get a bit of first-team football under your belt and see what it's like somewhere else.'

'I dunno, Dad ... I think they want to get rid of me.'

'No, son, don't be silly. They just want to toughen you up a bit. What did Ferguson say to you?'

'He said it would do me good and make me stronger. He said I could go there just for games and keep training with United in the week.'

'No way, son ... If you're going to go, you're going to go properly. You go there and train because if you don't all the players will resent you. They'll look at you as a big-time Charlie and you'll really get some stick.'

I helped convince him it would be a good idea to go to Preston. So he went back to Alex Ferguson and told him he'd be happy to go, but that he wanted to go there full-time.

On the Sunday night before he was due to go to Preston, I spoke to him again.

'You all right, mate?'

'Yeah, I'm OK, Dad. A bit nervous about tomorrow but I'll get through it OK.'

'Look, just go in there, do what you've got to do, get your head down in training and you'll be fine.'

On the Monday, I was as nervous as him because none of us knew what to expect. I couldn't stop thinking about him and about what he might be doing. I spoke to him later and he told us about his first day.

'I think I did OK, Dad, but I felt so embarrassed.'

'Why was that?'

'I got there and I didn't really know where to go or what to do. I found my way to the changing room and the manager, Gary Peters, just stood in front of all the other lads and said, "Right, this is David Beckham, who's here on a month's loan from Manchester United. He'll be taking all our free-kicks and corners from now on." It was so embarrassing. Anyway, we went out and trained and it was a really good session. I really enjoyed it but when I came in I just took off my kit and threw it in the middle of the dressing room floor.

'I got showered and changed and was just on my way out when the kit man called me over. "Dave, what are you doing?" I told him I was just on my way home. He said, "Well, what about your kit?" I looked at him and didn't really know what he meant. Then he said: "Sorry, boy, we don't wash your kit here, you've got to take it home and get it all done yourself." '

I think that was probably the first time he'd ever had to take his kit home and get it washed. But, to his credit, he got it all cleaned and dried ready for the next day, although I think his landlady probably helped out.

His first game for Preston was a friendly and Sandra and I were all set to go up for it. But he rang up and said he was only going to be playing half the game and it wasn't worth us travelling all that way. We took his advice but I wish we hadn't because he came on and scored a fantastic goal, which I've still got on tape.

His first proper game was against Doncaster in the League and David was due to be on the bench. We were determined to be there, so we drove up, collected David from his Manchester digs and then carried on over to Preston.

It was our first time at the club, but the reception we received was phenomenal – everyone was just so friendly. We were met at the door and David went off to join the team. Sandra and I were shown up to the directors' lounge and Tom Finney, the legendary Preston and England player and club president, introduced himself to us. I couldn't believe it – another one for the autograph book.

Then we went out to the stand and sat down to watch the game. Ironically enough, David was up against one of his old team-mates from Ridgeway – Ryan Kirby, Steve Kirby's boy. He'd got himself a contract at Doncaster and was starting that day.

David came on and really made himself a hero at Deepdale by scoring direct from a corner in a 2–2 draw. That doesn't happen very often in professional football but to do it on your debut – well, it was just another chapter in the fairytale. There were a few of his mates there from United to watch, Gary Neville, Chris Casper, Ben Thornley, Mark Rawlinson – that really meant a lot to him because he'd grown up with them.

He ended up playing five games for Preston … and we went to all of them. I've still got them all on tape, just as I have almost all his games.

At the end of the month, he went in to see Gary Peters, who was full of praise for him. He told him he'd been superb for the club, had a brilliant attitude and that all the players had really taken to him. His last game for Preston was against Lincoln and every single player came out and had a word with him and wished him all the best. David Moyes, now manager at Everton but then the Preston centre-half, said: 'Well done, David. It's been a pleasure having you at the club and we all wish you could stay.'

Gary asked David if he wanted to stay till the end of the season, which David was keen to do. He'd really enjoyed the experience and knew it was doing him good so he said he would ask Alex Ferguson.

David went back to The Cliff and plucked up the courage to knock on the manager's door – I think it was probably the first time he'd ever asked to see the boss. He was nervous about doing it but he was keen to stay at Preston. He calmly told Fergie that Gary had asked him to stay and, if it was all right, he'd like to give it a go.

Fergie just went mad. He slammed his fist on the desk and shouted: 'You're not f***ing well going anywhere. You're f***ing well staying here and that's the end of it.'

David was pretty upset but he knew better than to argue and just turned and left the office.

That evening he rang us and told us about his conversation with Fergie. I was about to hit the roof when he suddenly said, 'I'm playing, Dad ... I'm in the squad for tomorrow's game against Leeds.'

There was silence – I could hardly believe what he'd just told me. He was in the squad? For the game against Leeds?

Eventually I just said: 'No, you can't be.'

'I am, Dad ... it's true. I'm in the squad.'

Fergie hadn't told him during their meeting, preferring to let David find out when the team sheet was put up on the notice board.

Of course, that explained why Fergie had reacted so furiously to David's suggestion of another loan at Preston. But his decision to put David in the United squad had left us gobsmacked. Another sleepless night lay ahead as the nervous anticipation built up.

We left for the game at about 7am to arrive in Manchester by 10am. We hated being rushed and always left ourselves plenty of time to get parked and sorted out. We went off to the Chester

Court Hotel, where a lot of United's London supporters meet on match day, to have a drink and something to eat.

As kick-off approached, I was getting more and more nervous, fidgeting in my chair and desperate to get to the ground. Still we had no idea whether David would be playing from the start or just on the bench.

This was before mobile phones, so we only found out he was starting when a message was passed to us about half an hour before kick-off.

The nerves got to me straight away. It felt like someone had grabbed hold of my stomach and twisted it. Horrible – I felt physically sick.

Not only was my son making his debut for United – the club he and I had supported all our lives – but he was doing it against Leeds United, probably our biggest and most hated rivals. Games between the two teams are often very hard, with tackles flying in and no time or space to take a breather. I didn't have any doubt that David would be able to cope but there would certainly have been easier games in which to make your debut.

Sandra and I watched the game from the family enclosure, although I hated sitting next to her at matches. Usually, if she was sitting at one end of a row, I'd sit at the other because we just wound each other up. She would be worried for David and then have a go at me for muttering under my breath about what he was doing right or wrong. I have to admit I do talk to myself during games – and swear to myself as well, especially if he isn't playing very well.

But I hated talking to anyone during a match. I just wanted to concentrate on watching my son and trying to think of ways to improve him. Right from very early on Sandra and I made a pact to sit as far away as possible from each other.

I can still remember seeing him walk out on to the pitch, wearing the brilliant red shirt of United, as part of the team. It was a boiling hot day and Old Trafford looked fantastic. And the atmosphere was incredible, just as it always is for games against Leeds.

There is an underlying hostility and a real passion among the fans. David walked into that cauldron as though he belonged there and seemed right at home. To look at him, you'd never have thought he was nervous. But I knew that, just like me, he'd hardly slept the night before and that he'd been to the toilet countless times before kick-off.

Seeing him make that long walk out of the tunnel and on to the pitch is still one of the proudest moments of my life. People had been coming up to me in the couple of hours before kick-off, telling me how well he was going to do and how they were sure he'd be OK. But I didn't want to hear any of that – I didn't want people telling me how my son was going to play. I just wanted to watch it for myself and make my own judgement, just as I'd done from day one.

So there was anger, there was pride, there were nerves. I like to think I'm a strong man but the tears flowed that day, just as they did for Sandra. This was it, another milestone and another vindication of everything we'd worked so hard for. It was incredibly emotional.

In truth, the game was a scrappy 0–0 draw but David did pretty well. He played one lovely ball to Ryan Giggs, from which the Welshman had a volley saved by the keeper.

After the game, I saw David and I struggled for words to explain just what I felt about it. I just went up to him, gave him a cuddle and a kiss as always, and just said: 'Well done, mate. That was brilliant.'

Another piece of the David Beckham jigsaw had fallen into place but the picture was far from complete.

FROM FIRST TEAM TO FRANCE 1995-1998

'Sandra and I went to every game of that 1995–96 season – the season in which David, aged just 19, really became a United player. He cemented his place in the first team and played a key role in their success.'

Sandra and I became addicted to football, and especially to David's career at Manchester United. We fed that addiction week after week.

That first Premiership game against Leeds became the launch pad for everything David has achieved. He made the bench for the FA Cup Final at the end of that 1994–95 season but didn't come on. At least he got the special Wembley shirt, which I had framed and which still hangs on the wall above my stairs.

But it was the following season which finally revealed just how good David could be – and how good this United team could be. They came from 12 points behind Newcastle at Christmas to win the title on the final day of the campaign – and then complete the double by winning the FA Cup with a dramatic victory over Liverpool.

Sandra and I went to every game of that 1995–96 season – the season in which David, aged just 19, really became a United player.

He cemented his place in the first team and played a key role in their success.

Several games stick in the mind – a 3–0 win over Bolton which saw David stop dead in the middle of a run, then chip the ball up for Paul Scholes to score; a 6–0 win over Bolton in which United ran riot, with David, Nicky Butt, Paul Scholes, Steve Bruce and Andy Cole all scoring; a 2–1 win at Blackburn in August 1995 in which David scored the winner; and a 5–0 demolition of Nottingham Forest in the penultimate game of the season in which David scored two goals.

It was after the win at Blackburn that we first became aware of David's new-found fame. We were out shopping with him in Manchester and complete strangers were coming up to him and saying: 'Well done, Becks'; 'Great goal, David'; 'Let's have another one like that next week.' Of course, that was just a taste of what was to come and we just enjoyed it for what it was – proper United fans wanting to support one of their young lads.

The whole team was a pleasure to watch – Paul Scholes, Nicky Butt, Ryan Giggs, Steve Bruce, Gary Pallister, Denis Irwin and, of course, Peter Schmeichel. Ferguson had created a brilliant blend of youth and experience in a team which was full of self-confidence.

They clinched the Premiership title by beating Middlesbrough 3–0 on the final day of the season, with goals from David May, Andy Cole and Ryan Giggs.

As the team celebrated after the match, Ferguson sought out David, put an arm round his shoulder and said: 'This is a trophy we can win for years to come. We can win medals for another five years.'

There were a lot of comparisons with the Busby Babes because United seemed so good and were playing mind-boggling football.

I've still got all those games on video, just as I have all of David's games for United. If the game was on TV, I'd get Lynne to record it. If we missed it for any reason, I'd buy a copy as soon as it came out.

It's a great record to have and I love watching them over and over again. It's quite a collection now but it's a permanent record of everything he's achieved in the game. I'd like to think I can hand them on to him and he will one day sit down with his own sons and watch a few of them.

Of course, winning the title was just the first half of a momentous achievement – the double. Ever since Spurs became the first club to win both the League title and the FA Cup in 1961, the double has become the Holy Grail of English football – the achievement by which you measure all the others. I know it's been done more often since the Premiership started, but it's still the true hallmark of a great side.

United's Cup run that season is summed up by the March semi-final against Chelsea at Villa Park, which is definitely in my top six all-time matches.

Sandra and I had started the day by driving up to Manchester in the early morning, travelling past Aston Villa's ground on the way. It might seem crazy but we were desperate to savour the whole atmosphere of the day and wanted to be on the coach taking parents and club officials down to Birmingham from Old Trafford. We wanted to feel as much part of it all as possible. United looked after us all so well – we were taken to a hotel for a meal before the game and we really felt the buzz of this massive match.

As I took my seat next to Neville Neville, the nerves had really got to me. Everyone else seemed to be talking about the game but I preferred to stay quiet in the build-up to a match. I watched as David and the other lads went through their warm-up on the Villa Park pitch.

It was a strange United team, made up of many of the kids who had won the Youth Cup four years earlier. Besides David, there were the Neville brothers, Nicky Butt and Ryan Giggs. Both Steve

Bruce and Gary Pallister, United's massively experienced central defensive partnership, were out injured, so it was left to the inspirational Frenchman Eric Cantona to lead the side.

The game was incredibly open from the word go. It seemed the United lads were determined to play with the same carefree approach which had brought them so much success in lesser games. And Cantona was awesome – he really led from the front and inspired everything United did.

Even so, Chelsea were no pushovers. They had Mark Hughes, the old United striker, in their side and he seemed intent on making his old club rue the day they let him go.

He was instrumental in putting the Londoners ahead, barging past David after 35 minutes and crossing for the Dutch international Ruud Gullit to head powerfully past Peter Schmeichel.

Even though United were behind at half-time, I never felt we would lose the match. It's hard to explain but sometimes you just know your team will win – and that was exactly the feeling I had as the teams went in at half-time. Of course, I didn't dare tell anyone what I was thinking but I was pretty confident.

And that confidence proved well-founded in a second half which saw United tear into Chelsea with flair and passion. Within ten minutes of the restart, we were level. Cantona, of course, played a vital role, heading on Phil Neville's cross for Andy Cole to smash the ball home.

All the United fans roared as the celebrating players wheeled away and I joined in, urging the team to go on and achieve the win they so richly deserved.

Every dad must have wondered what it would be like to see your son score the winner in a massive game – well, this was the day I first found out.

Just four minutes after the equalizer, Chelsea midfielder Craig Burley tried an ambitious scissor-kick back to his keeper but the ball broke to David. He went past Terry Phelan and then sidefooted the ball home to put United ahead.

My emotions went into overdrive. I stood and cheered wildly as the players gathered around David and he soaked up the acclaim. It was a wonderful moment and one which still sends shivers down my spine today.

Chelsea did their best to get back, with Schmeichel pulling off one spectacular save from Gullit and Cantona heading John Spencer's late effort off the line. But it was too little, too late.

As the referee blew for full-time, Neville leapt to his feet and gave me an enormous bearhug, lifting me clean off my feet and almost toppling us both over the edge of the Villa Park stand. Unbelievably, incredibly, my son had put United in the Final!

We went back on the coach to Manchester that night and the team had a bit of a do in a city centre hotel to celebrate reaching the final. All the players were coming in and everyone seemed to be talking about my son ... Becks this and Becks that. It was an amazing feeling. I couldn't keep still – and we still had the Final – against Liverpool – to come a few weeks later.

Even though Wembley is no more than ten miles from our front door, we wanted to start the 1996 Cup Final weekend in Manchester. So we drove up to David's house on the Friday night and then came back to London by train on the Saturday morning.

Again, it might seem a ridiculous way to do things but we were so swept up by everything to do with Manchester United that we wanted to be part of everything on the day. As I've said, football – and United – had become the centre-point of our lives.

United had organized a special train, a bit like the Orient Express, for all the players' families and staff to travel down to London. We all had a compartment each and we shared ours with David's girlfriend at the time, a lovely girl from Liverpool called Helen.

We were met at the station in London and taken to the Royal Lancaster Hotel. We checked in and then got on a coach for the short journey to Wembley.

I was quite nervous outside the stadium because I'd got a handful of tickets for various people and had to wait for them to arrive before I could go inside. As so often at Cup Finals, it was a baking hot day and I was getting quite annoyed because time was getting on and still not everyone had turned up.

I eventually got to my seat just a few minutes before the teams came out and I'm so glad I did. I know a lot of parents have seen their sons come out as part of a Wembley Cup Final team, but that was a first for me and it was incredible. The wall of noise as they emerged from the tunnel, the managers looking so confident, the players tense and there, standing in the middle of it all, my son looking magnificent in his Cup Final strip.

I'd been to Cup Finals before, but nothing could compare with this. I'd seen my son play in all those games but now this was it – the biggest game of the season, played in front of a massive worldwide audience. My mind drifted back to those days back at Ridgeway Rovers, all the long hours we'd spent together on cold winter evenings practising and practising, and I felt so proud of what he'd achieved.

There were more tears, of course, and I don't mind admitting that.

David played so well in that final, as did all the kids. People claim it wasn't much of a game but I saw it more as two good teams almost cancelling each other out. I've watched it several times on video since and the technical quality of the players is very high. Maybe you see things differently when your team and your son are playing but I never tire of watching the game.

David had one magnificent shot, which he struck perfectly, but the Liverpool goalkeeper David James pulled off a superb fingertip save to stop his side going one down. Eric Cantona, who was really inspirational for David, led from the front, setting a magnificent example for the younger players around him.

The key moment came with just four minutes to go, when United got a corner. Of course, David took it and aimed the ball high into the penalty area. As it floated over, James came out and tried to punch it but didn't really connect. The ball cannoned off Ian Rush's shoulder and fell perfectly for Cantona to volley home.

The next four minutes took an eternity to go by and my nerves were jangling throughout. I never felt United deserved the win and one goal is never enough to guarantee victory. I sat motionless as the seconds ticked away, desperately willing the referee to blow the final whistle.

When it eventually came, I just sagged forward as the nervous tension drained away. As I watched the players celebrate, I could barely take in what my son had achieved. He had helped his club do the double – win the Premiership and the FA Cup.

I tried to express it to people standing nearby but the words wouldn't come out. I watched him and his team-mates climb the steps to the Royal Box and as he took his turn to lift the Cup, an amazing roar from the United fans went up. The tears welled up again and I watched the lap of honour through a misty haze.

After the game, we were bussed back to the Royal Lancaster for the mother of all parties, when everybody let their hair down.

We went in with Helen and were sitting on the same table as the Neville family. I was in my element, chatting away to all the players and enjoying every moment. David has said I was almost too overwhelmed to speak to him properly and he's probably right. It was a heck of a night.

At one point, all the players and the manager were called up on stage and all given a musical instrument. David had a sousaphone and others had trumpets, clarinets and more besides. It's just as well we'd had a few drinks, because they all had to do a turn on the instruments and none of them could play so it must have sounded awful. Then we had photographs done with the two cups and the medals, with all the family.

David went up to Cantona and said, 'Eric, I just want to say thanks for everything you've done this season and for the help you've given me.'

Cantona replied, 'You listened, you looked, you learned, you won it.'

And that was all he said. But that was enough and it made a powerful impression on David.

Life had become a little easier for Sandra and me during the season because David had just bought his first bachelor pad – a spacious four-bedroom townhouse with a garden close to United's training ground. It was great for us, because it meant we had somewhere to stay when we went up and David was always glad to have us around. It was also great for him because it was very near to where Ryan Giggs, one of his best mates, was living.

That was where we stayed when we eventually got back to Manchester after the Cup Final party. I can't remember what time we finally fell into bed but it was pretty late, so it was a heck of a shock to hear a loud 'bang, bang, bang' on the front door at about 8am.

We couldn't work out what was going on at first, so David leaned out of an upstairs window to see who it was and what they wanted. When he popped his head out, he found four burly policemen standing on the doorstep below.

'David Beckham?'

'Yes,' he answered.

'Sorry to interrupt you so early on a Sunday morning, sir, but we believe your car has been stolen.'

David invited them into the house and listened as they told the story.

'I'm afraid we've just found the car, a couple of miles away. It's been completely stripped. The wheels have gone, the CD player, the steering wheel. They were just starting to take the engine out when we arrived and scared them away. We're on to them now.'

Then it dawned on David. 'My car?' he said. 'It can't be my

car, because mine is still in the garage here and that hasn't been touched.'

'It wasn't a silver Ford Scorpio with a Cosworth engine, was it?' I said.

'Yes, sir, that's the one.'

'Great,' I said. 'That's my car.'

We'd left it on the driveway while we were at the Cup Final and they'd taken it over the weekend. So that was a pretty miserable end to a fantastic weekend but at least the police all went away happy – all four of them got David's autograph.

We spent many weekends that season staying at David's house after games. We'd either take him out for a meal or stay in to look after the place, while he went out with his mates.

There was one night we stayed up but I bet David wished we had gone home. He went out for the night and we were fast asleep in bed by the time he came home. We were woken up by the most terrible crashing and banging as he stumbled into the house. By the time we'd got up, he was being sick in the toilet.

'How many drinks did you have tonight?' I asked.

'Oh, only two or three, Dad. I think it must be a bit of food poisoning.'

'I'm not sure about that – you sure you haven't had too much to drink?'

'No, Dad, honest. It must be the food. Oh, I feel so sick.'

'I don't think so, son. I reckon it's the beer.'

But I have to say that was a very rare event. He was usually very careful about what he ate and drank.

He was developing some expensive and exotic tastes as well, which I suppose he could afford now he was on a full professional contract. When he decided he wanted a dog, he didn't want a Labrador or an Alsatian – it had to be a Rottweiler.

I remember going with him to collect the dog from the breeder. Of course, when he'd first seen the litter, the dogs had been tiny.

They were still quite small when we went back but as soon as we got through the door I could see these dogs were a handful.

While David went off to choose which one he wanted, I asked the breeder if I could meet the stud dog.

'Are you scared of dogs?' asked the woman selling them.

'No,' I answered. 'No problem with them at all.'

'OK. But when I open the door, whatever you do keep your hands by your side and don't make any sudden movements.'

I didn't know what I was letting myself in for and suddenly I was regretting my bravado. When she opened the door, this huge dog was standing there. I'd seen Rottweilers before, but this guy was enormous. He had a massive neck and he looked like he could eat me for dinner.

The dog came in and prowled round me. 'Just let him sniff you,' said the woman. 'And he'll be fine.'

I did as I was told. Then, in a voice which could only have been directed at the dog, she said, 'Stand up.'

With that, he reared back on his hind legs, put his paws on my shoulders and looked me straight in the face. He was huge – and one heck of a scary dog. But that was what David wanted – a dog that would look after him. The woman said the dog was trained to attack anyone who came near her and I'm sure she was serious.

When David came back, he couldn't decide which puppy he wanted – so we ended up taking two home with us. They sat in my lap as David drove us home. They turned out to be two of the most docile dogs you could imagine. They would let you do anything to them but, luckily, we never found out what they would do to a burglar.

David celebrated the double by coming away on holiday with us to Malta. We'd started going there when David was 15 – our first foreign holiday – and the whole family loved it. We were treated like royalty by the United fan club in Malta and one of Alex Ferguson's closest friends, Joe Glanville, lives out there.

He looked after us really well and was very kind to us. We've gone back there pretty much every year since.

It was during 1995 that David first signed up with the agent who represented him throughout his Old Trafford career – Tony Stephens.

We hadn't really bothered about agents when David was first starting out at United. We'd signed that first contract when David was 14 without consulting anyone. To be honest, we were so delighted he was playing for United that the money and other benefits weren't an issue.

We'd had a couple of meetings with agents around that time but hadn't really clicked with any of them. At the suggestion of one of the other parents at United, we met Mel Stein, who represented Paul Gascoigne at the time.

Sandra and I were shown into his office in Southgate, both feeling quite nervous because we hadn't had much experience of that world. We told Mel what David was like and what his hopes and ambitions were; how he hoped to go on and play for England and how he wanted a successful career full of trophies and medals.

Mel just looked at us and said, 'I reckon you should ask for a signing-on fee of £26,000 and make sure you get it. Tell Ferguson what your demands are and don't sign until you get them.'

When we came out, I said to Sandra, 'Can you imagine what Fergie's reaction will be if we do what he's just said?'

'Yes,' she said. 'We can't do that.'

Then, when David went up to Manchester full-time, a woman agent introduced herself to us. I've forgotten her name but I think she was the daughter of a friend of Alex Ferguson's. She said she wanted to represent David and made all the promises under the sun – all the usual stuff, big-money contracts, big-money sponsorship deals – but somehow we didn't feel she was right.

I think she was just starting out in the business and we wanted someone who really knew their way around and could really handle negotiations properly.

David's first sponsorship deal was with a boot company called Cica, who paid him around £6000 to wear their products. I think that was something he pretty much set up himself when he first turned pro.

But as his profile increased, it was obvious he needed someone to represent him. More and more offers were coming in and it was important to take all that hassle off him so he could concentrate on his football.

I think Tony Stephens introduced himself to David in Manchester and he made a good impression instantly, not least because he already represented David Platt, Alan Shearer and Dwight Yorke.

Tony was a former accountant but really seemed to have David's best interests at heart. He didn't see him just as a way to make money but genuinely wanted to help him develop all parts of his career. David felt really comfortable with him and that was the most important thing. I think David had pretty much decided to go with Tony but he invited me up to meet him before finally signing on the dotted line.

I know Ferguson was none too pleased to hear David had got his own agent but, obviously, David was keen to make sure he made the most of his career. From that point on, Tony took care of all the negotiations over contracts with United and sponsorship deals. In fact, after that first contract I've never known how much David has earned – I've never really thought it was any of my business. Obviously, he's on a lot more than £29.50 a week now.

The 1996–97 season kicked off with the goal that made David a household name – the wonder shot from the halfway line against Wimbledon. Even though Sandra and I were sitting almost in a straight line behind the point from which David shot into the goal, I didn't get much of a view of it.

It was a scorching hot August day and United were cruising at 2–0 up with just seconds to go. Brian McClair knocked a short pass to David in what looked like a fairly harmless position just inside the United half. As soon as he got hold of the ball, I could see what was in his mind – a carbon copy of the goal he had scored against Everton in a youth game a few years earlier.

Doing it in a youth game is one thing, but doing it in a Premiership match in front of TV cameras is another. As he shaped to shoot, I thought to myself, 'Oh, no, Dave, don't do that. You'll look a right idiot if that doesn't come off.'

But even before that thought had fully formed, David had hit the ball. As I watched it arc through the air, I was aware of the Wimbledon goalkeeper Neil Sullivan scampering back to his line, his eyes fixed on the ball.

Then, just as it was about to go in, the bloke in front of me stood up and raised his arms. I couldn't see a thing. The only way I knew it had gone in was from the reaction of everyone inside the ground. The place erupted – and I hadn't seen it. David May's dad was sitting nearby and he just shouted over to me, 'What an unbelievable goal – incredible.'

The goal was shown again and again on television and pundits queued up to tell the world how brilliant it was. But the praise which meant most to David came from his team-mate, Eric Cantona, who just said, 'Nice goal, David.' It doesn't sound much, but Cantona never gave much praise to anyone, so that was as good as it got from him.

Sandra and I made our way out of the ground and the only thing people were talking about was the goal. You could hear them all wondering how far out he'd been, where the goalkeeper had been, whether it was the longest shot in history. Of course, I was bursting with pride inside.

We waited outside the dressing room for David to come out. As he appeared, he beckoned us over and I gave him a big cuddle.

'Bloody hell, son – where did you get that from?'

But even as I asked him the question I could sense something wasn't quite right.

He looked at me and said, 'Dad, the boss has told me I'm not allowed to give any interviews about it. He doesn't want me talking to any of the papers, the BBC or anyone.'

'You what? You've just scored one of the most amazing goals ever seen on a football pitch, the sort of goal even Pele couldn't score, and you've got to keep quiet about it?'

'That's right, Dad. He doesn't want me to say a word.'

I couldn't believe Fergie would do that. It seemed so harsh on David not to let him have his moment of glory. I know David was upset but he had too much respect for Fergie to go against him. I suppose Ferguson knew what he was doing and he always tried to protect the lads from the media but, even now, that still seems to have been one occasion when he went too far.

I must have watched that goal 1000 times since and it gets better each time. It proved David had something special; that he was different from other players and that he would really go on to make a name for himself. It showed he had a quick footballing brain, that he could see things other players couldn't. It also proved he had the technical ability to do very difficult things on a football pitch. It's a shame he didn't score it at Old Trafford, but I suppose you can't have everything.

Within a few days of the goal, the new England manager Glenn Hoddle was due to announce his squad for the first World Cup qualifying game against Moldova in Kishishev.

There was plenty of speculation in the papers about whether David would be called up for the first time and he was desperate to play. He was round at our house when he found out he was in the squad. He and Sandra called up the squad on teletext and his name was there.

I was working in a hotel on the Edgware Road when he rang to tell me the news. I can't pretend it was a complete surprise but it was thrilling to hear it confirmed.

'How are you, Dad?'

'I'm fine, David. How's things with you?'

'Great, thanks – I'm in the England squad.'

'You're what …? Oh, fantastic, mate. That's brilliant.'

To be honest, I was lost for words. Being selected for your country is the crowning moment of any player's career. I must admit I was left pretty speechless by it – all fathers must secretly hope their sons will one day play for England but to see it come true was wonderful.

I was working on my own, so I didn't have anyone to pass the news on to. I was just in a daze, on cloud nine and I couldn't think straight. But after I'd hung up from David, the phone didn't stop all day and people kept coming in to congratulate me.

Once the shock had died down, we started to look at ways of getting to Moldova. To be honest, we had no idea where it was – I don't think many England fans did. The game was only a fortnight away and we looked at ways to get out there but the logistics were a nightmare. The FA did not organize an official trip and David advised us not to go because it was far from certain that he would play.

Of course, he did play and I have to say it's one of my biggest regrets that I wasn't there for his England debut. The game was on a Sunday afternoon and the whole family sat glued to the television, kicking every ball with him.

England, with David playing alongside Alan Shearer, Paul Gascoigne and his United team-mates Gary Neville, Gary Pallister and Paul Ince, cruised to a 3–0 win. It was a great way for David to start his England career and he went on to play in every game of that successful qualifying campaign for World Cup 98 in France.

The goal against Wimbledon and an encouraging England debut had kick-started a media frenzy. The papers were comparing the goal to other great goals in football history and suddenly David's name was being mentioned in the same breath as Pele, George Best and Johan Cruyff.

It was fantastic for me to think that my son, who was still only 21, was being ranked alongside those legends but it was another, more modern icon who made a bigger impression on him.

Sandra and I were both there the day David met his future wife, Victoria Adams, better known at the time as Posh Spice. It happened in the players' lounge at Chelsea after United had drawn 1–1, thanks to a sensational 90mph volleyed goal from David.

At the time, Victoria was far better known than David. The Spice Girls were at the height of their fame and she couldn't go anywhere without being mobbed. David was becoming more and more well-known but could still go out for a meal without too much hassle.

Sandra and I were in the players' lounge after the match, chatting with David, who looked really good in his collar and tie, club blazer and smart trousers. We could see Victoria on the other side of the room but were stunned when her manager, Simon Fuller, brought her over and introduced her to us all. I can't remember what David said but it wasn't much!

I was amazed that someone as famous as a Spice Girl, a pop star, actually wanted to speak to my son. She was very polite and seemed really interested to meet us all, although it was obvious that she was especially interested in David. We made a bit of small talk with her and then sidled away to leave her and David time to chat.

She made a very good impression on all of us but suddenly it was time for David to go. For away games, the players are all told what time they need to be back at the coach and they get in big trouble if they're late. So when that time came, David just had to say: 'I'm sorry but I have to leave.'

We always went down to wave him goodbye but I was surprised to see Victoria standing alongside us as the coach pulled out. As we were waving, I saw her looking up at him and waving to him on the coach. I could tell all the players were taking the mickey out of him about his new girlfriend but he took it in his stride – he was always able to give as good as he got.

The next time David and Victoria met was a few weeks later at Old Trafford when United played Sheffield Wednesday. Again, we were all in the players' lounge after the game. David walked in and Victoria made straight for him. They started chatting away and I've since found out they swapped numbers and that was the start of the relationship which seems to have fascinated the world ever since.

I can't pretend we were totally thrilled that David was going out with a pop star. We weren't worried about Victoria, it was more the sort of lifestyle someone in her world has to lead – going to clubs, staying out late, sleeping-in in the mornings. It is all the exact opposite of what a professional footballer's life should be. But our concerns were only the natural worries of any parent when their son or daughter starts a new relationship.

Even if we'd disapproved, it wouldn't have made any difference. David is as stubborn as I am and once he's made his mind up, that's it – he's going to go through with it.

I remember when he wanted to buy his first Porsche. He was offered the chance of a free Jaguar through his agent, Tony Stephens, and that sounded great to me. But he insisted on buying a Porsche. I just couldn't see the sense of that – splashing out a huge amount of money on a car, when you were being offered something just as good for nothing.

But he wasn't going to be put off by me. I had a bit of a go at him but there wasn't much point. In fact, my views probably only made it more likely that he'd go and get the Porsche. I'm sure the same would have been true if we'd said anything to try to put him off Victoria.

After winning two titles in a row, I suppose United were due for a bit of a slump and it came the next season – they allowed Arsenal to do the double in 1997–98. But by the time the Londoners had been crowned champions, all eyes were on the forthcoming World Cup, with many people thinking that England had a great chance of lifting the greatest prize of all.

The World Cup campaign opened with Glenn Hoddle's now infamous training camp, at the end of which all the players were called in individually to discover if they'd made the final squad. It was heartbreaking for those left out – especially Phil Neville and Paul Gascoigne – and I know David was upset for them. It was never his style to criticize the manager but I know he thought that situation could have been handled more sympathetically.

Glenn was one of David's heroes when he was growing up. In some ways, he had tried to model his game on Glenn's – the wonderful close control, the ability to hit long, accurate passes, the powerful shooting. But unfortunately the respect he had for Glenn all but died during the World Cup.

David was the only England player who played in every qualifying game, but when it came to the tournament Hoddle chose to discard him for the first game. It was bitterly disappointing.

There was one training session in France during which Glenn was working on free-kicks. Well, everyone in world football knows how good David's free-kicks are but Hoddle insisted he wanted the ball flicked up for David to hit. Not surprisingly, they were going here, there and everywhere. At the end of the session, David's final volley finished nearer the corner flag than the goal and Hoddle just walked up and said, 'I thought you were a quality player.'

None of the players could believe it – and nor could David. He was stunned by that remark and I know it really hurt him.

Sandra and I flew over from Stansted for every game, going out in the morning and flying straight back after the final whistle. That meant we didn't see David face to face at all during the tournament and had to make do with the phone. Of course, we were used to that because David had been up in Manchester for so long.

The first game was against Tunisia and I couldn't believe it when David called to say he wasn't going to be playing and that he'd be on the bench. Glenn had told David that he wasn't focused.

I've never heard so much rubbish in my life – I didn't agree with what he said and I didn't agree with what he did. I was so upset for David because there was no doubt he was focused – he wanted to win that World Cup more than anything. No one really understood what Hoddle meant and I'm still not sure anyone understands now. All David had ever lived for was football and to be at a World Cup was the highlight of his career.

He was very low after that, really down, but David didn't say anything about Hoddle. If the same thing had happened to me, I'd have been calling him all the names under the sun but that wasn't David and never has been.

Of course, England won the first game 2–0 with goals from Alan Shearer and Paul Scholes so I suppose Hoddle could say he was vindicated. Then he left David on the bench for the second game against Romania. But Paul Ince was injured early in the first half, so David came on early.

He had a fair enough game but we lost 2–1, after conceding a 90th-minute goal, which really put the pressure on us for the final qualifying game against Colombia.

Given all that had happened, we were pretty surprised when we got the call from David to say that he'd be playing against the Colombians. But after Darren Anderton put us ahead midway through the first half, we took control of the game.

David performed brilliantly in that match and scored an amazing goal from a free-kick – his first for his country – to help us into the quarter-finals against Argentina. It was wonderful to see him do that and both Sandra and I were thrilled for him. I could feel the relief as the ball hit the back of the net – the perfect answer to Hoddle's criticism. After that performance, there was no way Hoddle could leave David out for the Argentina game.

We were there, of course, sitting behind the large fences which still surrounded the pitch at St Etienne. There seemed to be pockets of Argentinian fans all over the ground, mixed in with the English, and the atmosphere was tense and hostile. It seemed the whole nation was wrapped up in this game – the papers had been full of it for days, with coverage on both the front and back pages. Whenever England met Argentina memories of the Falklands War were dragged up, which only added to the aggressive mood.

I suppose we should have guessed it would turn out to be an incredible night when Argentina took the lead after just six minutes. The England goalkeeper David Seaman made the slightest contact with Diego Simeone inside the box and the referee, Denmark's Kim Nielsen, immediately pointed to the spot.

Gabriel Batistuta powered the spot-kick home but just four minutes later England were level. As if to even things up, Nielsen awarded us a penalty when Michael Owen fell under a challenge and Alan Shearer did the rest. The England fans roared their delight and the atmosphere really started to throb. We all knew we were lucky to be present at a game which, whatever the outcome, would go down in football history.

Within seven minutes we were ahead, thanks to a sensational goal from Owen, who was just 18 at the time. He picked the ball up miles out from goal and just ran at the heart of the Argentinian defence, beating two men before crashing a right-foot shot into the net. As the players celebrated wildly, I glanced up at the scoreboard: Argentina 1, England 2 – we couldn't have asked for anything more.

But just seconds before half-time we were brought crashing down to earth when England conceded a free-kick just outside their own penalty area. Juan Sebastian Veron threaded it through to Javier Zanetti, who scored with a left-foot shot past Seaman.

It was a bitter end to a pulsating 45 minutes of football. To have come from behind to take the lead and then throw it away – all the football emotions were there and we went through them all. Part of me was delighted that we'd scored twice against a side tipped as possible world champions, but part of me was upset that we'd thrown away a lead.

David had been influential in the first half, making crucial runs and passes and always threatening danger whenever he had the ball. It seemed, to me at least, that the stage was set for him to play an even more important role after the break.

Then, early in the second half, I saw David get knocked over by a tough tackle from behind by Simeone. David ended up lying face down on the ground. I saw the referee move in and was convinced he was going to book Simeone. Then I saw David's leg flick up but I had no idea it had gone anywhere near an Argentinian.

We were utterly stunned when the referee pulled the red card from his pocket and brandished it at David. We could not believe what we were watching and as David walked towards the side of the pitch, Sandra looked up at me and just asked, 'Has he been sent off?'

'I think so,' I said. 'But I've no idea what for.'

It all happened so quickly and the atmosphere in the ground was so intense, that it was impossible to take in. The rest of the game passed in a blur. All I could think about was how David must be feeling. I wanted desperately to be with him but that was impossible.

Of course, everyone knows that Argentina went on to win a penalty shoot-out after extra time and claim their place in the semi-finals, leaving the whole of English football to wonder what might have been.

At the end of the game, we were obviously bitterly disappointed. What made it worse was that Sandra and I had to make our way past clumps of celebrating Argentinians as we walked round to meet up with David and his team-mates.

We were desperate to get there quickly because we knew David would be upset. Sandra and I were taken in by a few FA officials but, almost unbelievably, as the distraught England players came out, the Argentinian team bus pulled up outside and all their players were laughing and jeering at us. Some of them were standing up and twirling their team shirts jubilantly around their heads. That made it a million times worse.

When David eventually appeared from the dressing room, he was crying his eyes out. I put my arm round him, gave him a kiss and tried to find the words to comfort him. I just said, 'Don't worry, mate – it's only a game of football.'

But he was inconsolable, utterly devastated. If I could have taken him home there and then, I would have done. He couldn't find words to express his feelings – he just let us hug him. Of course, Sandra was in tears as well.

'Don't blame yourself,' I kept saying to David, 'it's one of those things. It could have happened to anyone.' But he wasn't really able to listen or take in what I was saying. As long as I live, I never want him or us to go through another experience like that again.

All the England players were there, along with their families. I think Neville Neville came up and gave David a kiss but no-one was saying much.

Then Hoddle came out. He just walked straight past us without saying a word. I couldn't believe it. Not a single word.

It was later on TV and in the papers that he came out with the quote which still leaves a bitter taste in my mouth now: 'If we'd stayed 11 against 11, we might have done something.'

What Hoddle did to my son was unbelievable. He knew David felt humiliated, embarrassed and ashamed of what he'd done. Yet instead of coming out in support of him, he blamed him – and no manager should ever do that. David was just 23 at the time, a young player who needed support and guidance – he didn't get either from Hoddle.

I still respect Hoddle as a player, but not as a manager. He hung David out to dry and that is something I can never forgive him for. He opened up the can of worms that was exploited by the media over the following few weeks and months.

Tony Adams was the one person who came out of that situation with any credit. He walked off the pitch and straight into the dressing room, where David was crying his eyes out. Tony sat down next to him, put an arm round his shoulder and said: 'Don't worry, David. We love you. You're still a great player and we love you. It's just one of those things.' I have so much respect for him for doing that.

From the moment we came out of that ground, our lives turned into a complete nightmare. I don't think anyone could have predicted quite how things would take off, how David would be turned into a hate figure or, more importantly, how strong he would have to be to fight back. With the benefit of hindsight, I think I can say this experience really turned David into a man. He grew up because he had to.

We had to come back to England that night, leaving David on his own with the squad. It was the last thing we wanted to do but we had no choice. We landed at Stansted at about 2.30am and just didn't know what to expect.

We came home and I watched the game again on television and I still couldn't believe what had happened. David has never really been able to explain why he flicked out his foot – it was just a heat-of-the-moment reaction by a young player caught up in the huge pressure of the occasion. Having said that, I still think David's offence warranted no more than a yellow card. The referee had made a huge mistake – but if he was holding the gun, Hoddle pulled the trigger.

I went up to bed at about 6am, knowing I'd be unable to sleep. I dozed fitfully until, at 7.30am, there was an insistent banging on the front door. I looked out of the bedroom window and couldn't believe what I saw. Our road, which is barely wide enough for two cars to pass, was full of more than 30 photographers, at least three camera crews and more reporters than I could count. It was bedlam.

I stumbled downstairs to answer the door – it was a reporter. I didn't even hear his question but just mumbled: 'No, I've got nothing to say.'

We'd had a few contacts with the media at various points in David's career up to then but nothing on this scale. We were terrified and just didn't know what to do.

Sandra and I were both supposed to be going to work and Joanne to school. But we couldn't even get out of the house.

Then we had problems with our phone lines. I had two lines into the house, one cable and one a normal phone line. We kept the cable one for our business use and the other one for normal, day-to-day stuff. I thought it was the right thing to do at the time but I learned a harsh lesson.

Sandra used the cable line to phone the old people's home, where she worked as a hairdresser. She told them she wouldn't be able to get in because of the problems we were having with the press. About half an hour later, the matron from the old people's home rang again. She wanted to know if Sandra had given the number to anyone because there were a load of reporters up there asking questions.

Then Joanne used the same phone to call a school friend and explain she wouldn't be going in. About twenty minutes later, the friend rang back to say he'd had a couple of calls from papers asking if he was related to the Beckham family.

We found out the next day that a van with an aerial had been parked in our road all day and one of Joanne's friends had seen two men inside twiddling dials. I'm certain they were listening in to our phone calls because when Tony Stephens, David's agent, rang the next day I told him my suspicions. By the time I got off the phone, the van was moving away.

With Tony's help, we made arrangements to meet up with David at Heathrow. He was desperate to join Victoria in America, where she was on tour with the Spice Girls. Tony had sorted out a private room for us at the airport where we could have about 45 minutes with David before his Concorde flight to New York.

We had to leave the house at about 2.30pm to get to the airport but as we left, so a whole posse of reporters followed on behind. It was like a scene out of a cops and robbers film – I was weaving in and out of the traffic to try and lose them, but they did their level best to keep up. It was crazy and very dangerous. I did U-turns, jumped over a set of lights by darting up the inside of a car which was stopping and went round roundabouts two or three times just to try and shake them off.

Eventually, I made it on to the M25 and thought I'd lost them. But when we got to Heathrow, there was another huge gang of reporters and photographers. They were shouting questions and taking pictures as we walked through the airport. It was a complete nightmare.

When we finally got through to see David he looked terrible – pale, drawn and utterly exhausted. He hadn't slept at all and was just desperate to get away to America and be with Victoria. We talked briefly about the game but then he just said:

'I've got some news, Dad, about me and Victoria.'

'Yes, mate?'

'I'm going to be a Dad. Victoria's having a baby.'

We didn't really know what to say. Of course, we were thrilled at the thought of him becoming a father but he'd known Victoria for less than a year and they were living their lives so much in the public eye, that we were worried about the future.

'Don't you think it's a bit soon, son?' I said.

'These things happen, Dad.'

We were with him for about three-quarters of an hour but he was very subdued and didn't really want to talk much more. We hugged him and tried to put his mind at rest, assuring him the England fans would forgive him and that a holiday would put him back in the mood for football.

British Airways had promised they would take David out the back way, to avoid the media scrum, but that didn't happen. Instead, he was marched straight through the airport and he had to run the gauntlet of the world's press. That was very tough on him but at least he was soon back on Concorde and away to see Victoria.

When we got back home, the press were still there. They'd spoken to our neighbours, other members of the family and were desperately trying to find anyone who knew David. For the whole of that week, the reporters were there virtually round the clock, constantly asking the same questions: Have you spoken to David? What did he say? How is he? When's he coming home? Is he going to leave England and play abroad?

The papers absolutely slaughtered David and I still find it hard to believe they were so hard on him.

Then we had another phone call from Tony Stephens. He said David had been in touch and he wanted to send us away on holiday for a week, because of all the aggravation. We were pleased, but not surprised. That was typical of David, to think of us at such a difficult time.

But we asked Tony what David's plans were. He said he was due back from America later in the week and was planning to go straight up to Manchester.

We knew what sort of reception he was going to get, so we told Tony not to bother with a holiday for us. We were going to spend those first few days with David, to try and protect him from the raging storm.

We met David at the airport. We even took his two dogs with us to help cheer him up. The police kept everybody away so we were given a pretty clear run through, although there were a few photographers as we came through customs. But we managed to get through. David and Sandra jumped in the Range Rover, while I followed behind in my car.

When we stopped at a service station for petrol and something to eat, loads of kids came up to David and were really great to him. It was obvious they didn't blame him for England going out of the World Cup – instead, they wanted to praise him for everything he'd done. It was a great boost for him and for us. He signed a few autographs and seemed to perk up a little.

But when we got back to Manchester, it was obvious things weren't right. We had a bit of a heart-to-heart that evening. He was very upset by everything that had been in the papers.

'I can't believe it, Dad,' he said. 'They want to blame me for everything.'

'That's the way it goes sometimes, son,' I replied. 'You've just got to go out and prove them wrong on the pitch.'

'Did you see the picture of my effigy on the gallows in the paper? It was hanging outside a pub. I can't believe it.'

'Yes, I saw that. But they're just idiots. They don't know what they're talking about. You've got to try to ignore it – it isn't easy, I know but you've got to try. Me and your mother are always here for you and you know that. Don't worry about it.'

He said Alex Ferguson had rung a couple of times while he was in America and been really brilliant. Fergie had had a go at Hoddle for the way he handled the situation, which David thought was great. And Fergie had just said to him, 'Come home now, David, and we'll look after you. Everything will be fine once you get back here. We'll support you all the way and take care of things.'

The next morning we woke up early. David had already been given a few extra days off by Fergie, so he was due in for the first day of his pre-season training.

As we sat round the breakfast table, he looked drawn and distracted, unable to concentrate on anything. It broke our hearts to see him like that.

'Are you all right, mate?' I asked.

'No, not really, Dad ... I feel really nervous.'

That was the first time we'd ever heard him say that before a training session. He was worried about everything – the reaction of the players; the reaction of United; the reaction of the press; the reaction of the fans.

'You go into The Cliff now,' I said. 'Get in that dressing room and the players will be brilliant with you. Trust me.'

We looked out of the window and there were about twenty photographers and reporters out there. We knew we'd have to face them at some point but David wanted to drive out in his Porsche, which was in the garage. I went down to move his Range Rover, which was blocking the driveway, to leave a clear run for him to get away.

As I was moving that, David dashed out, opened the garage door and climbed into the Porsche ... which wouldn't start. He tried a dozen times to get it going, with the world's press looking on, so you can imagine his embarrassment as the cameras flashed away.

In the end, he had to give up on the Porsche. He jumped out of it and into the passenger seat of the Range Rover to let me drive him into training. But as we got nearer and nearer to The Cliff, so he got more and more nervous. He was really worried about what the players might say and it was breaking him up inside.

I tried to reassure him again. 'They'll be fine, mate. They're all your friends – they'll stick up for you. Give it five minutes and everything will be OK.'

After the session, he was totally different. The nerves had gone and he looked great.

'How did it go?' I asked.

'It was great, Dad. I really enjoyed it. Can you believe what happened? As soon as I walked into the dressing room all the players started diving to the ground and flicking out their legs. I just stood there and laughed.'

That was all it took to put him right – a bit of mickey-taking in the dressing room.

We stayed up there for the rest of the week and he got better each day. The crowds of reporters and photographers started to dwindle and he got more and more confident.

The defining moment of his recovery came in the first game of the season at Old Trafford against Leicester.

We went to the game as usual but we didn't know what to expect. The press were still pretty hostile so there was no way to predict how the fans would react to David. He felt a lot better in himself but there was no way he could judge what reception he would get.

When he walked out into the August sunshine, the Old Trafford fans all started chanting his name and cheering. It was a very emotional moment for all of us.

But you couldn't have written the script for what happened in the game. Unbelievably, Leicester went 2–0 up before Teddy Sheringham pulled one back for United, heading home from David's shot. Then, in the 94th minute, United were awarded a free-kick just outside the box. The crowd went silent – there was only one man who was going to take it – my son. I have never heard Old Trafford more quiet or felt a more eager sense of anticipation there.

Of course, David scored, curling a fantastic shot around the wall to earn United a point. The place erupted and you could see just how much it meant to him. After the nightmare of the World Cup, he was back at home, back with the people he loved and ready to inspire his club to a season they would never forget.

THE TREBLE
SEASON
1999

'Even though we always sat with the United fans, we could hear what the opposition fans were chanting and it was very painful. When you hear 30,000 people abusing your son, it makes your blood run cold.'

He had to put up with a hell of a lot of abuse in the early months after the World Cup. He was booed at every ground and some of the chants and taunts were really vile. It was particularly bad at West Ham, where the fans seemed to have a special hatred for Manchester United and he needed a police escort to get into the ground. The Leeds fans were also particularly hateful, jeering every time he touched the ball.

Some mindless idiots even threw things at him but he tried very hard not to let it affect him. I think the way David dealt with it all helped him grow up. He realized he had become a huge celebrity and had to find ways to cope with that. He got pretty low at times because sometimes it seemed only the United fans liked him. But I was very proud of him for coming through that experience a better player and a stronger man. The United fans really stood by him and that was fantastic. They were brilliant to him and to us.

Sandra and I found it much harder to deal with than David. Even though we always sat with the United fans, we could hear what the opposition fans were chanting and it was very painful. When you hear 30,000 people abusing your son, it makes your blood run cold.

I have to admit there were times when I reacted in ways I shouldn't have done. At Leicester that season, we were waiting outside the ground with some friends to wave the players' coach off. Standing alongside us was a huge fat bloke in his forties, wearing shorts and a Leicester T-shirt about twenty sizes too small, with his wife. As the team bus appeared, this bloke started hurling abuse at the players, saying how rubbish Gary and Phil Neville were, that David wasn't fit to wear the England shirt and that anyone and everyone connected with Manchester United were scum.

I'm afraid I just lost it. I'd had enough. I went up to him and told him to leave it. He took one look at me and said, 'What's it got to do with you?'

'You're having a go at my son and I don't like it,' I replied.

'Well, tough, mate ...'

With that, I laid into him and we started brawling in the car park, trading blows in full view of the players. I was dimly aware of them all crowding round to look out of the window while me and this bloke were going for each other.

Eventually, Paddy Crerand and Steve Bower, who were there with MUTV, managed to separate us and the bloke walked away, although he still turned round to give us a few V signs as he went.

As I was dusting myself down, my phone went. It was David.

'Did you hit him, Dad?'

'Yes, I gave him a whack.'

David whooped with delight and shouted out, 'He's hit him, lads, he's hit him.'

I heard the cheer in the background as the news spread through the coach.

That's not the only time I've had to step in to defend my son and the team he plays for. I never advertise the fact that I'm David's dad and, because I'm nowhere near as good-looking as him, people rarely pick me out as his father.

That saves me from a lot of grief and I do try to turn a deaf ear when people start going on about David but it's not always easy. Everyone seems to have an opinion about him, even though they don't know him.

A couple of years ago, I had a row with a woman at work. She was a Chelsea fan and she went on and on about United's kids, about how they weren't good enough and how they'd been mollycoddled too much and that they all earned too much money.

Then she started having a go at David and I wasn't having that.

'Do you know him?' I asked.

'No, not to speak to,' she said. 'But I can tell exactly what he's like. I think he's a right prat.'

'What makes you say that?'

'Oh, it's the way he comes across. I can't stand him.'

'Do you know him?' I repeated. 'Have you met him?'

'Well, no. But you can tell what he's like. He's so flash.'

'How can you say that?' I said. 'Look, I meet people all the time and you can't judge anybody until you've met them, can you? I can tell you people who are rude, people who are sarcastic, people who are horrible but David Beckham doesn't come across like that, does he?'

Then another woman piped up: 'Well, I think he's lovely!'

So I took my chance with the first woman. 'There you are, that's what she thinks and she doesn't know him either. Why do you say something horrible about someone you've never met? That is someone's son you're talking about. What would you do if someone said that about a son of yours?'

'I'd have a right go at them.'

'Exactly – so don't have a go at my son.'

She had no answer to that and just stood there open-mouthed. She had no idea I was David's dad but that really shut her up.

I get that sort of thing a lot, sometimes from people who don't know who I am and sometimes from people who do.

Some people have a go at the way David looks – at the way he changes his hairstyle every five minutes, the clothes he wears or his tattoos. All I can say to them is that it is his body – if that's what he wants to do, then fair enough. I can't say I like all his hairstyles and I certainly wouldn't wear the kind of clothes he likes.

As for the tattoos, I've got three myself and had my first one done when I was only 14. I went with an older cousin, who was also having one done.

I was so scared of what my parents would say that I had 'Best Mum and Dad' tattooed on my forearm. I went home with my sleeves rolled down but somehow my mum knew. And she went mad when she saw it, calling me all the names under the sun and warning me of what would happen when Dad found out.

I was determined to keep it a secret from him, so I walked round with my arms completely covered for the next three weeks. But he was out working on his car one morning, when he asked me to give him a hand to lift something. I didn't think twice about it but as I leaned in to grab hold of the engine, my sleeve pulled back.

'What the bloody hell is that, you stupid little bastard.'

He gave me a massive whack around the head and kicked me back in the house. And I always had to keep it covered when he was around – he hated it.

Of course, that didn't stop me getting more done. I've got another one on my right bicep, which says 'True Love Sandra', and another on my left arm of an old-fashioned sailing ship.

I remember David getting his ears pierced, which I wasn't happy about at all. He was 15 and all his mates were getting their ears done. I called him an old tart and told him he was turning into a poof, but he wasn't bothered. It wasn't something I liked but I didn't have much choice.

I used to stick up for all the young players at United. There's been criticism of just about all of them at some stage – both the Nevilles, Nicky Butt, David – but it's usually from people who don't know what they're talking about. I've lost count of the number of arguments I've had in pubs, restaurants or just when I'm out and about defending these guys. They are all quality players and one bad game doesn't alter that.

Those lads had plenty of opportunity to prove just how good they were in that 1998–99 season as they cruised to the Premiership title. One of the best games was an 8–1 victory over Nottingham Forest, in which David played out of his skin and Ole Gunnar Solskjaer scored four goals in February 1999.

With things going so well at United, David was doubly pleased when a new England manager, Kevin Keegan, was appointed. Glenn Hoddle had been forced to quit as England boss after some crass remarks made in the press and Keegan came in. I knew David would respond well to Keegan's special brand of coaching. Keegan would encourage him, gee him up and get him going.

After just one coaching session before England's European Championship qualifier against Poland in March 1999, David was buzzing when I spoke to him.

'It was fantastic, Dad, really good. He just kept encouraging us all the time. There wasn't a word of criticism, it was all so positive.'

That was great to hear after the disappointments of the World Cup and everything looked good for the qualifying campaign for the Finals to be held in Holland and Belgium in 2000.

The League title was always the priority for United but the FA Cup campaign went just as well. The game everyone remembers is the astonishing semi-final replay against Arsenal, after the first game had ended in a 0–0 draw.

It was played at Villa Park, just as the amazing semi-final against Chelsea three years earlier had been. That should have been a good omen but nothing seemed to ease the tension on that cold March night.

Incredibly, David put United into the lead after just 17 minutes, hitting a superb shot from 25 yards past David Seaman. As the ball slammed into the back of the net, I leapt to my feet and punched the air in delight – but I knew there was still a heck of a long way to go against an Arsenal side who were chasing the double just as hard as we were chasing the treble.

The action flowed from end-to-end and United never looked totally comfortable, so it was no surprise when Dennis Bergkamp scored an equalizer for Arsenal after 69 minutes, his shot taking a huge deflection off defender Jaap Stam to beat Schmeichel.

It looked as though the tide had turned in Arsenal's favour and that feeling was reinforced just four minutes later, when United's inspirational skipper Roy Keane was sent off for a bad challenge on Marc Overmars. As soon as Keane flew in on the tricky little winger, we knew he was in trouble.

That meant United had to play the last 20 minutes with just 10 men against one of the best teams in England. Arsenal threw everything at United – it was horrible to watch. I felt it was just a matter of time before they clinched the winner and could hardly bear to look.

My worst fears were realized in the final minute, when Arsenal were awarded a penalty. Bergkamp stepped up to take it but, incredibly, Schmeichel made an amazing save to take the game into extra time.

The only thing I remember about that extra time was Ryan Giggs's amazing winning goal. He picked the ball up on the halfway line, ran through five Arsenal tackles and then smashed the ball past Seaman. Giggsy was one of David's closest friends at Old Trafford and the image of him wheeling away after scoring, twirling his shirt above his head, will stay with me for ever.

It was an astonishing goal and a fitting end to a fantastic match.

As the final whistle went, I just felt enormous relief that we had come through such a severe test. If we could do that, maybe we could do anything.

That put United into the Final, which, after the semi-final, was something of an anti-climax. United beat Newcastle 2–0, with goals from Teddy Sheringham and Paul Scholes, and the result was never in doubt. That feeling of anti-climax was reinforced by the very subdued celebrations that night – everyone was saving themselves for what turned out to be one of the greatest nights of all our lives – the European Cup Final against Bayern Munich at the Nou Camp stadium in Barcelona.

Sandra and I went to every game of that European campaign, home and away. It was a punishing schedule but an incredible experience for us.

We always travelled with the official United party, which meant flying out from Manchester Airport at around 6.30am on the day before the game. Since we lived 200 miles away, it often meant leaving our house at around 3am for the drive north. We always liked to get there early in the hope of seeing David or some of the other players at the airport.

It was fantastic for us to be involved. We hadn't been abroad even on holiday until David was 15, so all the travelling was still very exciting for us. The trips were organized down to the last detail – we were always met at the airport when we landed, bussed to our hotel and then given a few hours to look around before a drink and a meal in the evening.

We often slept late the following morning and would spend most of the match day relaxing in the hotel, before the game in the evening. Then we would fly straight home after the match, pick up our car and drive back to London. It was often 5am or 6am before we arrived home and we'd have to be up a couple of hours later for work.

I'm ashamed to admit there were times on that return journey down the M6 and M1 when my eyes would close and I'd feel myself falling asleep at the wheel. It was utterly exhausting but more than worth the effort for the thrill of seeing David perform on that stage.

We had a brilliant time on those trips and met some amazing people. One of the best was Frank Lammar, a famous comedian and female impersonator, who was a massive United fan and often joined us for away games.

He was a real larger-than-life character, who loved to be the centre of attention and was very well-known by people at United, including Alex Ferguson and many of the players. He had his own nightclub in Manchester and that was very much the in place at the time.

Frank never made any secret of his homosexuality but people on those United trips really took him to their hearts. Sadly, he died in 2003 and there was a huge turnout for his funeral in Bolton, including Fergie, Bryan Robson, Roy 'Chubby' Brown, Jeremy Beadle, Ryan Giggs's mum, and a host of entertainers and celebrities.

I remember a fabulous trip we had with him to Dortmund, a couple of seasons before the Treble year. We had eaten in the hotel and then gone down to the bar. Frank was taking charge of things as usual and had split us into two teams for a football quiz. There must have been about 15 or 20 of us. The drink was flowing and we were all having a great laugh.

There was a woman playing background music on the piano – I suppose she was in her fifties but beautifully dressed. Frank couldn't resist – as soon as he heard a song he recognized, he started singing and it wasn't long before he was sitting next to her, playing the piano. He started knocking out a few old favourites and it was developing into a really good sing-song when suddenly her hand moved over on to Frank's leg.

Well, the look on Frank's face was a picture. Then she started to snuggle up close to him on the piano stool, while Frank was doing his best to edge away.

I don't think Frank really knew what to do and eventually his only escape was to go up to bed. He slipped off, leaving us to carry on drinking deep into the night. Then, suddenly, Frank re-appeared in the bar.

'Hey, Frank, what you doing?' we shouted. 'Thought you'd gone to bed.'

'I had,' he explained. 'But then there was a knock on the door. I got up and it was the piano player, asking if there was anything she could do for me! I had to let her down gently and told her that wasn't my kind of thing.'

He told the story so brilliantly that he had us all falling about with laughter.

It wasn't always as much fun as that. We went to Turkey when United played Fenerbahce in October 1996 and it was one of the most terrifying experiences of our lives.

We hadn't enjoyed even arriving in Turkey. Our passports were scrutinized heavily and we all had to pay a special tax before they would let us into the country.

The game was tense and the atmosphere inside the ground was very threatening. The terraces were alive with hatred and violence, bright red flares were being set off all over the place and there was a deafening, blood-curdling roar from the fans.

David put United ahead and then Eric Cantona scored the second to give us a 2–0 win.

But when Cantona's goal went in, Neville Neville couldn't help himself – he leapt to his feet and punched the air in delight. One Turkish fan sitting behind threw a cup of coffee at us and was immediately shoved back into his seat by a policeman. Then a little lad of no more than ten aimed a series of V signs at us before turning round and baring his backside.

The worst part came at the end of the game, as we were being bussed back to the airport.

We had a journey of about half an hour but all along our route there were crowds of baying fans. And they were on top of every bridge, raining bricks, stones and lumps of concrete down on us. A window was smashed in the players' coach, near to where Phil Neville was sitting, and bricks hit all our coaches. It was very frightening and some of the girls were in tears. It was a huge relief to fly out of Turkey that night.

David saved some of his best performances in the Treble season for the Champions League – and those games gave us some brilliant memories.

We played Bayern Munich in the qualifying stages and, luckily enough, when we played them out there in Germany the annual beer festival was in full swing.

We were there with the usual crowd – Neville Neville and his wife Jill, Ron Wood, Kineally and Frank Lammar, and had a fantastic two days. Some of the details are a bit hazy, but we spent hours sitting in the beer halls watching giant German waitresses lug armfuls of foaming steins to our table. We must have tried every beer under the sun and then some.

David was outstanding in the 3–3 draw with Barcelona at Old Trafford, scoring one of the goals. Then, when United were drawn against Inter Milan in the quarter-finals he came up against Diego Simeone, the man who had wrecked his World Cup.

All the pre-match hype concentrated on their rivalry but I was immensely proud of the way David dealt with that situation. It would have been very easy to get caught up in all the nonsense, but he stayed focused and helped United win 2–0 at Old Trafford and draw 1–1 in Milan to go through.

In Milan, Jill Neville decided to go out shopping for the afternoon. She always had an eye for a bargain wherever we went and she loved haggling. She thought she'd hit the jackpot when she came back with not one but two Louis Vuitton bags. She'd only paid a few bob for them from a bloke on a street corner, so I'm not certain they were genuine, but she was made up.

We played Juventus in the semi-final, drawing 1–1 at Old Trafford thanks to a last-minute goal from Ryan Giggs. Then, in Turin, we went 2–0 down inside the first ten minutes and it looked as though the European Cup dream was over. No-one comes back from two down at the Stadio delle Alpi.

At least that was what we all thought before that night, which saw one of the greatest comebacks in European Cup or Champions League history. The memory of it still leaves me breathless.

I was so proud to be a United fan that night, so proud to see my club make another piece of history and so proud that my son was at the centre of it all. It would be unfair to single out David's performance on that night because if ever a performance epitomized the team spirit at the club, this was it.

There is no doubt that football can put you through the full range of emotions in just the space of a few minutes. As Juventus cruised into a 2–0 lead with two goals from Filippo Inzaghi, my heart was in my boots. We knew when we arrived in Turin it would be a tall order to go through because Juve had that vital away goal. But, even so, we didn't want to be humiliated.

But that looked a distinct possibility as the Italians stormed into a 3–1 aggregate lead. We were devastated and had all but given up hope. I kept looking down at David, hoping he could find that little spark of inspiration to launch a fight-back but, in my heart of hearts, I thought we were finished.

Then, just 14 minutes later, United won a corner and, of course, David jogged over urgently to take it. His pinpoint cross found the head of Roy Keane, who glanced it past the Italian defence to give United hope. We leapt to our feet but, even then, never considered a victory was possible.

But within ten minutes United were level on the night and ahead on aggregate, when Dwight Yorke headed in a cross from Cole.

The next hour of football was as tense as anything I've ever seen. Juventus poured forward, knowing they needed a goal because United's two away goals meant they were behind in the tie. We were like little children who hide behind the settee when the scary bits come on television – desperately wanting to watch, but being afraid to just in case anything awful happens.

The tie was a knife-edge for almost the whole of the second half but, with just six minutes to go, United made gloriously sure of victory when Andy Cole scored the third goal. From the depths of despair, we were now at the summit of joy – and all in the space of an hour.

It was an astonishing result – the only downside was that both Roy Keane and Paul Scholes picked up yellow cards which ruled them out of the Final.

We longed to see David after those games but often it wasn't possible. Occasionally, we'd see him at the airport but there wasn't much time to chat. We usually had to make do with snatched conversations on the phone as we made our way home.

Of course, all those memories pale beside the Final – still the most exciting game I have ever seen, or am ever likely to see.

We were staying in a very good hotel near the harbour in Barcelona, having flown out as usual the day before the game. But people seemed distracted and not really up for having a good time. The nerves and the tension of such a big occasion really got to everyone and nobody wanted to let their hair down.

The weather was fantastic so we tried to take our minds off the game by going out for walks along the seafront or up the famous Ramblas. We even got invited on to one of the yachts moored in the harbour but we were too nervous to appreciate the luxury and splendour. Everybody was only thinking about one thing – the game.

I spoke to David briefly about four hours before the game. I knew they would have a rest in the afternoon and got him just as they were getting ready for their team meeting.

'All right, Dave ... how are you doing?'

'OK, Dad ... I'll be glad when the game's started.'

'I know that, mate. Good luck, play well, do well – you know what I want.'

That was the phrase I'd sent him out with in almost every game since the Ridgeway days. He knew what it meant – work hard, never give up, play to the best of your ability, get your passing right and think of the team. That phrase crystallized everything we had spent all those hours working on back in Chingford – now I hoped it would help him win the Champions League.

We were taken by bus to the ground and had to leave about three hours before kick-off. Victoria was flying in for the game, so I left her ticket behind the hotel reception desk, so she could just drop her bags and head out to join us.

It seemed to take ages to reach the Nou Camp – and then the bus pulled up miles away from the stadium. All the time, my nerves were becoming more and more frayed. We had to get out and walk through about three police checks before finally getting through to the entrance. We met up with a few of the other parents, along with some of the legends of the 1968 European Cup winning team like Bobby Charlton. Then, just as we were being shown to our seats, my phone went.

'Ted, it's Victoria ... My ticket's not here.'

'Oh, no,' I said. 'It must be. I left it there a couple of hours ago.'

'Sorry, Ted ... It's not here. I've asked and they say they don't know anything about it.'

'I don't know what to say, Victoria. I definitely left it there – I'll try to sort something out. You go and get changed and I'll let you know.'

I was doing my best to sound calm but I doubt I succeeded. I was a bag of nerves and now I had this to sort out. In the end, Ned Kelly, the old Manchester United security chief, helped me big time. He made a few calls to the right people and got everything sorted out.

We finally took our seats about ten minutes before kick-off, with Victoria sitting between Sandra and me.

We were with all the other players' families in the middle tier of the vast Nou Camp, directly in line with where Teddy Sheringham and Ole Gunnar Solskjaer would make history. The towering stands rose above us on all four sides, so steep we wondered how people did not fall off them. It seemed three-quarters of the ground were United fans, with just the end to our right reserved for the Germans. And the noise was incredible as the two teams came out to line up for the pre-match presentations.

We were sitting in front of the United reserve goalkeeper Raimond van der Gouw and his wife, Marita. With five minutes to go and United still one down, Marita leaned forward and shouted in my ear: 'Don't worry, we'll win this match 2–1.'

I looked at her as though she were mad. I couldn't see any way we'd get back into the game and, to be honest, Bayern deserved to win it. They'd definitely been the better team on the night. But the game was being played on what would have been Sir Matt Busby's 90th birthday – and that had to be a special omen.

Of course, what happened next is the stuff of legend. Two David Beckham corners and two goals completed the most amazing comeback in European Cup Final history. As Victoria, Sandra and I hugged each other and jumped around manically, I caught Marita's eye and yelled: 'Blimey, you must be a witch!' Neville Neville was leaping around like a lunatic, Bobby Charlton was going crazy – it was just incredible.

It was bedlam after the game. Everyone was so happy and so disbelieving. I just wanted to get home and watch the game again and again – but first we had a party to go to. We made our way down to a lounge somewhere deep inside the Nou Camp, where some drinks and snacks were laid out. Then David came in, wearing his winner's medal round his neck, and he was more excited than I'd ever seen him. He was really buzzing.

'That was unbelievable,' I said. 'Well done, mate. I can't believe what you've just done.'

'Nor can I, Dad. It was amazing, fantastic. I can't believe it.'

There were more tears, not surprisingly, and then we went back on the bus to the hotel for another one of United's famous parties.

We were met by Tony Banks, the then minister of sport, Bobby Charlton and the other United directors. Then the players started to arrive in ones and twos, all still wearing their medals.

We went through to a large hall, where tables were laid for dinner. After we'd eaten, Alex Ferguson stood up to pay a glowing tribute to his team.

'This is the best group of players I've ever had,' he said. 'This victory proves how great a squad we have. It is the most amazing feeling I've ever had in football and they all deserve every bit of praise they receive.'

After that, the players really let their hair down. After all, it was the first time the club had won the European Cup since 1968. Everybody was up dancing, with the European Cup taking pride of place in the middle of the floor. We all had our photographs taken with it – Sandra and I had one with David, while the reserve team coach Eric Harrison made sure he got one with the whole 'class of 1992'.

It was one of the best nights of my life. We stumbled into bed at some stage but several of the players, notably Dwight Yorke, came straight off the dance floor and on to the bus to the airport in the morning. There were some pretty sore heads on that flight back to Manchester but no-one minded. The Treble had been won.

We flew back with the players and more than a million people turned out to welcome them home. We were on one of the coaches which toured the city, drinking in the cheers of the fans. It was astonishing to think we were in the middle of all that – and that our son was a key member of a team that would be remembered at Old Trafford for ever.

David's personal life seemed to mirror the success of his professional life. His first son, Brooklyn, was born in March on the night after David had faced Inter Milan and Simeone at Old Trafford.

He came into the world at the Portland Hospital – a very upmarket venue and a long way from Whipps Cross Hospital, where his father had taken his first breath. Sandra and I went in to see the new baby on the day he was born. Brooklyn was my first grandson and all the more special for that. As I held him in my arms, I couldn't help but think back to the first time I'd held his dad. It seemed like only yesterday, as I'm sure it does for a lot of parents, but so much had happened in those 24 years. If anything, I was even more nervous about holding Brooklyn.

As I cradled his tiny head, I wondered about his future and what part football might play in it. I knew he would have a very different upbringing to the one we gave his father, but I hoped he would come to love the game as much as David and I did.

David was much more of a hands-on father than I ever was. Right from day one, he was changing Brooklyn's nappies and he certainly did his share of the feeding.

But in the way he treats them now they're older, I very much see myself in David. He is a stickler for discipline, just as I was, and doesn't let the boys get away with much. I've seen him give Brooklyn a smack on the back of the hand when he's needed it and I don't think there's anything wrong with that. When he raises his voice to them, they know he means it and they step into line. He's in control of them and I'm sure he remembers his upbringing.

He loves being with his boys and cannot wait to be with them. He spends as much time with them as he can.

By the time Brooklyn came along, Victoria and David had moved. The townhouse in Worsley was a little too small and too exposed as their fame grew. Unfortunately, they had to become more and more concerned about security.

They bought a fantastic apartment in Alderley Edge, which was very secluded and private, and started work on their Hertfordshire home which has become known as Beckingham Palace.

But if that sounded impressive enough, we were all knocked out by their wedding in the summer of 1999. I can't remember the exact moment he told Sandra and I he was getting married but we were both thrilled, especially with Brooklyn on the way. I suppose all fathers look forward to their sons' wedding days – it's another rite of passage, another step on the road to manhood. But very few fathers will ever attend a wedding like David and Victoria's.

They took over a huge castle in Ireland – Luttrelstown – and we flew over the day before the wedding. David and Victoria had sold the first report and pictures of the wedding to *OK!* magazine. I have never seen security like it. There were three sets of guards just to get into the castle; then, once through the gates, there were more guards. They were all on walkie-talkies and were on patrol 24 hours a day for the whole weekend.

Mind you, they needed to be. Some photographers from the papers got dressed up in army fatigues and camouflaged their faces to try to sneak in at night. They were crawling along ditches and through the undergrowth to try to get under the barriers and snatch a quick picture. The guards even used heat-seeking night sights to spot where they were and deal with them.

I spent a good part of the weekend with my daughter Lynne's little girl, Georgina, who was born about a year before Brooklyn and was just a toddler at the time. But we weren't allowed to go outside into the grounds because some of the papers had hired helicopters to take aerial shots of the place.

The night before the wedding Sandra and I joined David, Victoria and her family to eat around one big, long table in the splendour of the hotel dining room. It was a wonderful night.

The wedding was incredible. We had to walk down the path to the small chapel, which was all decked out with flowers. It

CHURCH OF IRELAND

The Marriage

of

Victoria Caroline Adams

with

David Robert Joseph Beckham

at

Luttrellstown Castle

on

Sunday, 4th July 1999

at

4 o'clock

The order of service from David and Victoria's wedding in July 1999.

was gorgeous – a fairytale wedding. My little granddaughter and Victoria's sister's little girl were dressed up as fairies. I know all the pictures have been seen around the world but it really was as fantastic as it looked. Yet another day to remember, given to me by my son.

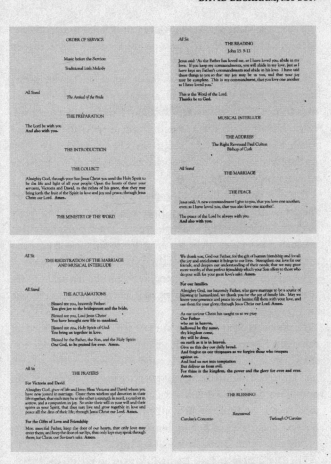

It's hard to describe my feelings on that day. David comes from a working-class family in Chingford – it's a heck of a long way from there to a fairytale wedding in a castle. Even in my wildest moments of fantasy about where his career might take him, I never imagined anything like that. And I certainly never dreamed that so many people would be so interested in every tiny detail of his life.

He's met so many people – the Queen, the Prime Minister, Nelson Mandela, Muhammad Ali. These people are absolutely at the top and he's met them.

For my son to get an OBE from the Queen before he's 30 is truly incredible. It just shows what an impact he's made and that makes me so proud. Yet, in some ways I shouldn't have been that surprised. David has always had a real ability to connect with people and touch them. That goes right back to when he was a little boy – even on the odd occasion he had misbehaved, he'd get out of it by being so sweet and charming.

I've seen him when he meets people and it doesn't matter whether they're men, women or children of any age, he can somehow relate to them. Obviously, a lot of people are starstruck and tongue-tied when they meet him but he has an ability to put them at ease and make them feel comfortable. We always taught him the importance of being polite and of having good manners and it's paid off. He never comes across as arrogant or rude and that's because he just isn't like that.

That was so clear when he used to arrive at Old Trafford on match days. Sometimes we'd go up to his house from London and then drive in with him to the ground. We used to arrive around midday to find hundreds of people waiting to get a glimpse of him or maybe even an autograph. It would take David twenty minutes or so just to get through them all but it was fantastic for him to feel so loved. He'd sign hundreds of autographs and then pose for photographs with some of the disabled fans.

Then we'd go in and see Kathy Phipps, who ran the reception desk. She'd been there for ever and had known David since he was 14. He'd always give her a kiss and a cuddle and she'd tell him what a lovely boy he was. It was great.

She also used to look after a lot of the fan mail. I can remember her opening up a cupboard door behind the desk to show us two full post-office sacks of letters, all of it for David.

When he first started getting famous, we used to take it home with us and try to deal with it. But there would be all sorts of stuff in it – cheques, underwear, little mementoes, cuddly toys.

The cheques were usually payment for television interviews David had done. He never bothered to chase any of the payments up – they just came. And we lost count of the number of bras and pairs of knickers that came through the post, usually with a letter promising David the night of his life.

We always tried to answer the letters and send out pictures. In the end it all got too much for us and Kathy, along with another couple of women, took care of it all.

A little of that celebrity has rubbed off on Sandra and me. If we had time to kill at Old Trafford before a game, we would often go down to the youth development office for a chat and a laugh. We used to see a lot of the parents whose boys were in the United youth set-up. They were carbon copies of what we'd been, nervously waiting there, constantly wondering if their sons were going to make it or not. A few of them came to us for advice but I always felt nervous about this: we'd been lucky because our son had made it – I didn't want to start telling other people what to do because no two boys are alike.

Children always react especially well to David. I remember we were at Leicester in the early days, watching David play in a reserve match. As usual, we waited in the foyer for him to come out of the dressing room. Suddenly, this little girl came up to us. She couldn't have been more than 11 or 12.

'Excuse me, are you David's dad?'

'Yes, I am,' I replied. 'What can I do for you?'

'Do you think he would sign an autograph for me?'

'Yes, I'm sure he would, no problem. Just wait here and he'll be out in a minute.'

David was happy to oblige when he came out but then the little girl looked up at him and said, 'Would you mind if we did a quick photograph with my brother?'

'No problem,' said David. 'Where is he?'

'He's just outside – he's in a wheelchair.'

David went with her and they had their pictures taken. This little lad looked really poorly in his wheelchair and David was very upset by it. He was desperate to help him as much as he could, so he signed a couple of photographs for him.

The little girl came up to thank David and gave him a peck on the cheek. You could see the tears start to well in David's eyes. She was so grateful for what he'd done but David knew it was nothing.

A couple of weeks later we got a letter from the little girl thanking us again and telling us how her brother had died a few days earlier. His last wish had been to have the photo David signed in the coffin with him.

David was deeply upset by that.

We used to get a lot of letters from people thanking us for the inspiration David had given to them or their children. It was very humbling for all of us but it's a side of David's fame you don't see very often.

There was another incident at Leicester, when David was warming up before a game, trying a few shots at goal. He hit this piledriver but it missed the goal and smashed straight into the face of a little boy sitting in the stand. His face just exploded with blood and David was horrified. He rushed over to apologize as people crowded round the lad to sort him out.

David made sure he saw the lad's father and asked him to bring his son round to the players' entrance at the end of the game. The St John Ambulance people cleaned up the lad and he came back out to watch the match.

After the game, David saw him and gave him his autographed boots as a way of saying sorry. Rather sadly, the lad sold them for about £3500 a few years later. He said he needed the money more than a souvenir.

The most heartrending situation I remember David dealing with was when we heard about two young brothers who were both diagnosed with terminal illnesses, one after the other. I read about them in a paper and discovered they were huge Manchester United fans.

I spoke to David and said it would be great if we could do something for them and he was more than happy to help.

I rang the paper and explained who I was. They thought it was a wind-up at first and refused to believe I was David's dad but eventually I convinced them. We got them match tickets for a game at Old Trafford and passes for the players' lounge. Sandra and I bought them a ball each from the Old Trafford shop.

It was heartbreaking talking to the lads' mum, learning how first one of her sons had been diagnosed with terminal cancer and then how his brother had come down with identical symptoms. They were desperate to meet David and, as we waited outside the players' entrance before the game, I kept telling them he'd be here in a minute.

When David finally pulled up, both boys burst into tears. They couldn't believe they were about to meet their hero and were totally overwhelmed by it. David came over and he was brilliant with them – signing autographs, pictures and stopping for quite a long chat with them.

It is times like that that put the whole of David's career into perspective. Our only ambition for our children was for them to be healthy and happy. We were lucky that was fulfilled but David's life has been the most amazing adventure and we've been so fortunate to be a part of it.

I sometimes think I'm going to wake up one day and someone will tell me it was all a dream. So many things have happened to him – good and bad – but there does seem to be some sort of script for it all. I'm not a religious man but I do feel there's someone or something up there guiding us.

FROM
THE TREBLE
TO TOKYO
1999-2002

'Sir Alex Ferguson is the most motivated, single-minded man I have ever met and I have enormous respect for him. I admire his insistence on discipline and firmly believe he gets the best out of all his players. That was certainly true of David.'

David and everyone connected with United started the new season on a massive high. With the treble under their belt, they felt almost invincible and were determined to prove it.

Sir Alex Ferguson was the driving force behind that desire. He is the most motivated, single-minded man I have ever met and I have enormous respect for him. I admire his insistence on discipline and firmly believe he gets the best out of all his players. That was certainly true of David.

If I and many other people did the groundwork, Fergie provided the finishing touches. Without Fergie's influence, I very much doubt David would have been half the player he has become.

It might be stretching a point to say that Fergie was almost like a substitute father for David but he certainly looked up to him. I think Fergie was more remote from him than I was, but nevertheless there were similarities. He was tough on David, just as I was; he wanted David to fulfil his potential, just as I did; he wanted to help David become a legend at Old Trafford, just as I did.

I'm David's worst critic. I don't just watch him play, I study the way he plays and I know when he's doing well and when he's doing badly. I'm sure Ferguson did the same and he knew far more about it than I did, so his views had to be listened to.

We got to know Ferguson pretty well in those early days. I went to several dinners with him and Sandra and I once spent a week on holiday with him in Malta. He is a difficult man to get to know but the harsh exterior hides a man who really cares about his players. He wants to see them succeed on the football pitch and doesn't want anything to get in the way of that.

His fears about David's lifestyle after he and Victoria got together have been well documented and I must admit I shared those concerns and spoke to David about them. I was worried when he bought the big house in Hertfordshire because I knew he would want to spend a lot of time there and that would mean travelling when he might have been better off resting.

I know Ferguson told David he was worried about that and you had to respect that opinion. After all, he'd just won the treble and was running the biggest football club in the world. He knew what he was doing.

Things came to a head in February 2000, when David phoned in to say he would have to miss training because Brooklyn was sick. I think Fergie felt Victoria should have missed work to nurse him and he went ballistic when David returned to training the next day.

That was tough for me to deal with because, deep down, I agreed with Fergie. I can remember David getting annoyed with me for supporting him.

'Why do you always stick up for the boss?' said David. 'You're always sticking up for him. Why?'

'Because he's right – if he's wrong, I'll stick up for you. But I've always said I'll be honest with you and that's what I'm doing.'

I think it was hard for David to accept criticism but I felt I had to say something. It was a tough situation for all of us, especially as David's rollercoaster relationship with the press had taken another downturn.

United had been forced to miss that season's FA Cup to take part in a world club competition, organized by FIFA, in Brazil. While the rest of English football was slogging through the cold and wet of January, David and United were lying on the beach in Brazil. It didn't make them very popular.

David made things worse for himself by getting sent off in a game against Necaxa for a high tackle. Once again, the press jumped on his back, branding him petulant and spoilt. I have to say, that was complete nonsense. It was certainly a bad tackle, as he admitted to me afterwards, but using it as evidence of his state of mind was utterly ridiculous.

I know David was very upset about not playing in the FA Cup, because he had been brought up to believe that was just as important as the League. He'd always looked forward to it and, obviously, it was the chance of another medal.

The United lads more than made up for the FA Cup disappointment with a devastating display in the Premiership. They ended up winning it by 18 points from Arsenal and finished the season being unbeaten in their last 14 games.

They seemed to score goals for fun that season – 97 in all, a Premiership record – and seemed so full of confidence after their Champions League triumph. I saw them beat Arsenal 2–1 early in the season, both Everton and Newcastle 5–1 and a crushing 7–1 victory over West Ham on April Fool's Day, in which David scored one of the goals.

That result as good as wrapped up the title more than a month before the end of the season.

It is hard to pick out a particular highlight because United were just so dominant. Whenever they took the field, they expected to win – for me, it was almost like watching Ridgeway Rovers again.

United's success that season was a great tribute to Ferguson's managerial skills because he somehow found a way to keep the players hungry, despite all the glory of the season before.

The one disappointment came in Europe, where United's bid to retain the Champions League trophy ended with a 3–2 defeat at Old Trafford against eventual winners Real Madrid.

Once the title was wrapped up, all attention switched to England's bid for glory in the European Championships.

Of course, England ended up needing to beat Scotland in a play-off to get to Belgium but the squad travelled out for the tournament full of optimism. That was especially true of David and the other United lads after such a dominant season.

Strangely, I think that success, and the success of the treble season, may be one of the reasons England didn't do as well as everybody had hoped at Euro 2000. Many of the England fans seemed to turn on the United players and made their lives hell. I can only think it was jealousy of their success but it seemed ridiculous that it should spill over into the international arena.

That was especially true of our first game in the Finals, against Portugal in front of 33,000 fans in Eindhoven. Sandra and I had flown out for the game and were sitting with Neville and Jill Neville. Both their sons, Gary and Phil, started the game, as did David.

I have never heard such a sustained torrent of abuse at a football match. It was utterly disgusting and seemed to be coming from everywhere, even from fans sitting very close to us. Most of it seemed to be directed at the Neville boys and how their parents put up with that I will never know. Sometimes fans can forget that the players have wives, children and families. I would love some of the idiots who shout these things to be put in the position where 30,000 people are screaming abuse at them.

As everyone knows, England lost the game 3–2, having been 2–0 up. The match ended with that famous picture of David, who had been the target for some of the vilest abuse ever heard at a football ground, giving the one-fingered salute to the England fans. We had been sitting on the opposite side of the ground to the players' tunnel so we only found out what they'd been chanting the next day when David rang us.

He sounded as low as I'd ever heard him – even worse than after the 1998 Argentina game.

'I can't believe it, Dad. They were saying things like "Your wife is a whore" and "I hope your baby gets cancer." What's the point of playing for England if they're going to start abusing my family? It's just not worth it.'

I had to agree with him. It makes you wonder what sort of sick people follow England. David didn't need all that, especially after everything that had gone on at the World Cup. I know he thought very seriously about quitting England at that time and no-one could have blamed him if he'd walked away.

I have to say that Keegan was brilliant with him and showed what a good man-manager he was. He defended David to the hilt. And when people heard exactly what the abuse was, they understood why David had reacted.

Of course, the tournament ended in failure for England, despite a 1–0 win over Germany in the second game. We lost 3–2 to Romania, our last group game, and we were on our way home – another English failure in a massive competition.

It was extremely disappointing for every England fan and, of course, for David. He had gone into the tournament with such high hopes and to come home without even having reached the knockout stages made it a miserable summer.

England's luck didn't improve the following season. Their first game was against Germany at Wembley in a qualifier for the 2002 World Cup. It will always be remembered as the game which forced Keegan to quit, unable to cope after a 1–0 defeat.

He had obviously been under pressure after Euro 2000 and felt he had no choice but to go.

I was in the crowd that day and knew David was struggling almost from the kick-off. He was carrying an injury but managed to get through about 70 minutes before being replaced.

The pain of seeing Dietmar Hamann slam a 30-yard free-kick past David Seaman in the England goal only made things worse and the whole country seemed to go into mourning as the final whistle went.

I didn't get a chance to speak to David immediately after the game and only heard Keegan had quit as I was driving home. I spoke to David about it later in the day.

'It was strange, Dad,' he said. 'He just came into the dressing room and said he was packing it in. We tried to talk him out of it but his mind was made up. He came up to me and gave me a hug and I wished him all the best for the future. But no-one really knew what to say.'

Just four days after that game, Howard Wilkinson took charge for a drab 0–0 draw in Finland, which David missed because of his injury.

I know David was upset by Keegan's departure but he had good reason to be thrilled when Peter Taylor took over as a stopgap before Sven Goran Eriksson's arrival.

Almost the first thing Taylor did as England boss was to make David skipper for the friendly against Italy in November 2000 – one of the proudest moments of David's life and one of the proudest moments of mine.

David called to tell us just before the announcement was made public and I was on cloud nine for the rest of the day. It didn't really sink in until I saw the pictures on television and in the papers of

Taylor handing him the captain's armband. I even had a little walk over to Chase Lane Park to see where it had all started and thought back to those very early days.

After everything that had gone before, I suppose I shouldn't have been surprised but I still had to pinch myself to believe it was true. My son was the captain of England. Another piece of the Beckham jigsaw had fallen into place, even if we did lose the game 1-0.

Once again, United were untouchable in the League, winning the Premiership by 10 points with a series of devastating displays including a 6-1 victory over Arsenal and a 6-0 win over Bradford. With three League titles in a row, Ferguson announced he would retire at the end of the following season.

I didn't really discuss that with David. Obviously, he'd had his problems with Fergie but he knew how important the manager was to United's success. But I think it's only natural that sons don't confide in fathers as much when they get older. That was certainly true of me and my dad. I liked to sort out my own problems and David is very much the same.

I must admit that David's relationship with Sandra and me had changed a little by this time. Obviously he was married so it was no surprise that he would want to confide in his wife rather than his dad. We spoke on the phone but, quite rightly, he was putting his wife and child first and gave them more of his time.

I think it's the same in almost all families – relationships between parents and their children change as the children grow up and become parents themselves. As you grow older, you tend to tell your parents less, partly because you don't want to trouble them and partly because you're not sure they will fully understand.

By the start of what should have been Fergie's final season, all our focus was on the World Cup qualifying campaign. After the upheaval of Keegan's departure, England were by no means certain to get through and that was certainly weighing on the new captain's shoulders. But he thought a lot of the new England boss,

Sven Goran Eriksson, and the two of them have a relationship based on mutual trust and respect.

I think David came of age as an England captain on one of the greatest nights in our recent history – the 5–1 victory over Germany in Bayern's Olympic Stadium – perfect revenge for the 1–0 defeat at Wembley. David skippered the side and gave a superb performance. He and the other players seemed to grow as the game went on – by the time the final whistle came they looked enormous.

It was an astonishing game played in an atmosphere like I've never experienced at an England match. The big Munich stadium is pretty impersonal and the fans are a long way from the pitch but that just seemed to make the England fans cheer all the louder.

The wonderful thing for all of us watching was that even though the Germans took the lead after just six minutes through Carsten Jancker, England hit back almost immediately through Michael Owen, who rammed the ball home after David's whipped-in free-kick.

We knew it was going to be a special night when England took the lead deep into added time at the end of the first half – again from one of David's perfect crosses. This time it was headed down by Rio Ferdinand for Steven Gerrard to slam home.

To score right on half-time is always devastating for the team that concedes – and the Germans were no exception. The second half was as good a team performance as I've ever seen from England. Owen, in particular, terrorized their defenders and it was no surprise when he completed his hat-trick. Emile Heskey added the final goal with more than 15 minutes left.

That allowed us all plenty of time to savour the victory and take maximum delight in putting one over on the Germans. It was a special night and breathed new life into our qualifying campaign.

I travelled to all the qualifying games home and away, always going on the official trips and always with the Neville family. The trips were superbly organized and, not surprisingly, the whole focus is the football. You are flown out, bussed to the hotel and you don't really have a lot of time for sightseeing, not that there's a great deal to see in places like Albania and Finland.

We had a good time in Greece, although we spent most of the day wandering the narrow streets around the Acropolis desperate to find somewhere for a drink and a meal. As usual, I was with Neville Neville and we eventually found a bar very near the stadium, so we spent the afternoon in there before walking up to the game. We won the game 2–0 and David scored with a sensational free-kick three minutes from time – the icing on the cake as far as I was concerned.

The qualifying campaign came down to the final game – the return against Greece at our beloved Old Trafford in October 2001.

Sandra and I had gone up the day before and were staying in the Marriott Hotel, along with the players. That gave us a welcome chance to see David before the game. We came down to the foyer and one of the FA security people directed us to the team room.

As we walked in, I just said, 'Hello, skip.'

He laughed and said, 'Oi, don't be cheeky.'

We gave him a cuddle and he said he was in great shape and looking forward to the game. I gave him my usual 'you know what I want' speech and we wished him luck.

Sandra and I had great seats for the match – front row of the second tier right on the halfway line. Even though David had taken a box for the game, we preferred to be outside in the middle of it all, soaking up the atmosphere. Nev was behind us and the whole crowd was buzzing with expectation. Everyone in the ground seemed to be supporting England and they all expected us to win.

David walked out holding the hand of little Kirsty Howard, from the Francis House Children's Hospice. She was a beautiful little girl but terribly ill and had to have her oxygen bottle wheeled alongside to keep her going. To see David taking such great care of her was wonderful, especially before such a vital match. He was so tender with her and walked out at her pace, making sure all the other players did as well.

David looked magnificent in the all-white kit – he looked like a giant and he played like a giant. Even now, I think it was the best game he ever played for England. In fact, it was probably the best game he has ever played. His work rate, his passion, his desire, his passing, his crossing – everything was working to perfection and he was an inspiration to the players around him, even if they didn't always seem to be on his wavelength.

England needed just a point and no-one outside Greece expected them to lose. But that wasn't the way the game panned out. England struggled to put together consecutive passes and it seemed the harder David worked, the more ragged the team performance became.

The crowd was stunned into silence when the Greeks took the lead through Angelos Charisteas after 36 minutes. Suddenly, the unthinkable seemed to be happening right in front of us. I can still recall the feeling of dread which crept up inside me.

The second half was little better. England somehow managed to grab an equalizer through Teddy Sheringham but gave away a second goal just a minute later. As the game drifted towards a nightmare defeat, it seemed only one man believed we could salvage the point we needed – David.

He was everywhere, making tackles, passes and urging on his team-mates in all areas of the pitch. It seemed to me that he had decided England were going to get the equalizer and nothing was going to stop him.

Of course, it came down to that free-kick deep in injury time. It was just outside the penalty area – normally his favourite position – although he must have had a dozen similar ones earlier in the match and none had come off. He told me later that Teddy Sheringham had asked to take this last one but David refused. He was happy to take the responsibility and believed it was his duty as captain.

When the ball hit the back of the net, the place erupted. I remember people around us in the stand openly crying, barely able to deal with the emotion of the moment. I have never seen anything like it at a football match. With one inspirational flash of brilliance, my son had taken his team and his country to the World Cup Finals. Yet again, the tears pricked my eyes. Another chapter in his amazing story had been written.

An hour or so later, we were waiting in the lounge at Old Trafford. When David walked in, it was as though he had taken over the room. He was high on the excitement of the day, still buzzing from the game and the magnitude of what he'd done.

'What can I say, son? You were absolutely awesome. That's the best game I have ever seen you play. Well done.'

'Thanks, Dad. I really enjoyed that. It was brilliant.'

'Whatever you had last night, make sure you have some before every game – and let me have some of it too.'

As we talked, the pop star Usher came in. I didn't really know who he was but I found out later that he had become friendly with David and watched the game from his box.

'Well played, man,' he said. 'That was the most amazing game I've ever seen in my life.'

We drove home that night and, as usual, I watched the game over and over again just to let it all sink in.

But if we were utterly elated by David's performance, one man was very keen to bring him down to earth – Alex Ferguson.

When David got back to Old Trafford, the first thing the boss said was that David had to keep working hard.

I think he was worried that it would all go to David's head – the captaincy, the success on the international stage, the fame – and that it would affect his performances for United. I think there was also the nagging doubt in the back of Fergie's mind that, having announced his retirement, he was worried the players might be tempted to take liberties because they knew he was going.

David had also been having problems with Ferguson over his new contract, problems which grew worse as the season wore on. It seemed the papers had nothing else to write about because every day seemed to bring another twist to the contract saga. That wasn't something I really discussed with David – he had Tony Stephens helping him sort out all the details and I knew these things were never sorted out quickly.

Having said that, I do believe it was a bit unsettling for both United and David to have the negotiations hanging over their heads all that year. As things turned out, it was a rough season for United. We ended it empty-handed and had to watch Arsenal do the double – never a good feeling for a United fan. It was even more galling that United could only finish third in the Premiership, three points behind Liverpool and 10 behind the Gunners.

United had gone out of the FA Cup in the fourth round, losing 2–0 to Middlesbrough, and their Champions League campaign came to a juddering halt against Bayer Leverkusen in April.

The one consolation was that David finally agreed the new contract right at the end of the season and it was finally signed in May, on the pitch before United's last home game of the season against Charlton.

The supporters cheered wildly as he put pen to paper, proof positive that an East London boy had been fully accepted by the Mancs.

By that time, though, there were major doubts over David's fitness with the 2002 World Cup Finals in Japan and South Korea looming.

He had got the first knock on his foot in April, when United played Deportivo La Coruna in Spain in the Champions League.

He played on with the injury but then ended up breaking a bone in his foot in the return leg a week later. That kept him out for the rest of the season and it was going to be touch and go whether he would even make the squad.

I could not believe the fuss that was made over this broken metatarsal – a word I only learned because it seemed to be in the papers every day. I suppose it showed just how important David was to England and how famous he was but the saga of that foot was utterly ridiculous.

One paper published a daily update on his foot, while another went even further. I couldn't believe it when a reporter knocked on my door one day, holding a huge picture of David's foot. He told me if I put my hand on it at midday he would help him get better quickly and be fit for the World Cup. I'd never heard such a load of old nonsense.

David was very upset about the injury and we spoke on the phone quite often in those weeks when his World Cup future hung in the balance. He did get very low because he really wanted to perform at the World Cup, especially after the horrors of France 98.

Mind you, I think he was even more upset when his great mate, Gary Neville, picked up the identical injury a few weeks later. There was no chance of Gary being fit for the World Cup and that was a hard blow.

If the build-up to the World Cup was dominated by the injury, the highlight was undoubtedly the Japanese party David and Victoria threw at their Hertfordshire home just before the team left. For splendour and luxury, it was right up there with their wedding. It was certainly a lot different to the Beckham family knees-ups my mum and dad had thrown when I was a kid.

We were greeted by Japanese girls in traditional kimonos and that theme continued throughout the evening. The food was Japanese, there were lanterns everywhere and it felt as though we'd already arrived at the World Cup.

The night raised a huge amount for charity, mainly due to a huge auction. A signed pair of David's boots went under the hammer and the bidding quickly got up to something well over £20,000, with two guys fighting it out. Then David stepped in and said he'd put up a second pair of boots, if they'd both call it quits and pay up.

There were quite a few celebrities there – Elton John, Ray Winstone, Lee Evans, Sean Bean, all the England players, Sven Goran Eriksson. I spent most of the evening talking to Lee Evans and his wife, plus Ray Winstone. It was a fantastic night and a great send-off for the lads.

I have to admit I was very reluctant to go to the World Cup. I've never been a good flier and the thought of 12 hours in an aeroplane was terrifying. I had a lot of work on at the time and I was worried about that as well. If I could have got out of going, I would have done but the trip was already booked, so I had no choice.

We flew over with a load of England supporters and I needn't have worried. We had a fantastic time on the plane, so much so that we drank it dry! They ran out of beer, wine and spirits and the stewardess told me that had never happened before.

I'm so glad I went – it was an unbelievable three weeks.

We landed in Tokyo and went straight to our hotel. It was about 1pm and Sandra and I were starving, so we went out to find something to eat with a few of the lads off the plane. At first, the only place we could find open was a sort of delicatessen in a petrol station and I didn't like the look of the food there.

We decided to carry on walking and one of the lads suddenly noticed some lights on at the top of a flight of stairs. We went up to have a look, opened the door and found ourselves in a restaurant packed with Japanese people.

We looked at them and they looked at us. We couldn't speak a word of Japanese and they couldn't speak a word of English. We mimed eating, so they showed us to a table and gave us a menu. Of course, it was all in Japanese and we didn't have a clue what we were looking at. So I started pretending to be a chicken, walking around flapping my arms and squawking – then one of the other lads pretended to be a cow, using his fingers as horns and mooing loudly.

Maybe the Japanese use different sounds for their animals because they looked at us as though we were mad. We were certainly the centre of attention but it looked like we were going to go hungry.

Then one of the other people in the restaurant came to our rescue. He had just enough English to translate words like chicken and beef. At long last, they twigged what we wanted and we ended up having the most fantastic meal.

As we were finishing, our translator came over and started talking to us again. We told him we were over for the football and eventually it came out who Sandra and I were. The reaction was amazing.

'You Beckham father?'

'Yes, I am.'

'You Beckham mother?'

'Yes,' said Sandra.

'Oh, fantastic. Great to meet you. Can we take picture?'

The whole restaurant stopped and looked at us. They all gathered round and wanted their pictures taken with us. It was like we were the King and Queen and for the first time I began to appreciate just what a worldwide figure my son had become.

Of course the tournament went brilliantly in the early stages, with a 1–1 draw against Sweden – David's first game since breaking his foot – thanks to a goal from his old Tottenham schoolboy team-mate Sol Campbell. David lasted into the second half but looked pretty angry when he was substituted.

Then it was the now infamous return against Argentina in Sapporo and the chance for both England and David to gain revenge for that horror night in France four years earlier. Once again, the fates conspired to put David at the centre of the action.

The only goal of the game came just a minute before half-time, after Michael Owen had raced into the penalty area and been chopped down by the Argentinian defender Mauricio Pochettino.

All the English fans in the stadium leapt to their feet, screaming 'Penalty!' No sooner had the yells been let out, than the referee was pointing to the spot.

There was only one man who was ever going to take that penalty. David never even considered the possibility that he might miss. He had – and still has – so much confidence in his own ability. I wish I had as much faith – I sat in the stand almost shaking with the tension as the crowd went silent and David placed the ball on the spot.

He turned to go back to the start of his run-up. No-one dared utter a word and the crowd seemed to hold its breath as he reached his mark. With one quick look, he ran towards the ball and connected with his right foot, as I willed him to hit the target.

It wasn't the best penalty he's ever hit – it went straight down the middle with power – but it went in. And that was all that mattered. You could say it was fate again but it takes a hell of a lot of nerve and technique to do that in such a high-pressure situation. It was wonderful to watch it hit the back of the net.

We didn't see a great deal of David during the tournament but both Sandra and I were there when he got back to the hotel after that match. We knew exactly what he'd been through, what we'd all been through, after that game in 1998 so revenge was very sweet indeed. Sandra was in tears and we both just hugged our son, thrilled and delighted yet again. I think all three of us ended up crying but there was no shame in that.

After the 0–0 draw with Nigeria in the sweltering heat of Osaka, we had to face Denmark in the second round in Niigata, a much more traditional town than Tokyo.

We'd met a couple from Middlesbrough who were on the trip with us and they invited us to have dinner with them on the night we arrived in Niigata. We decided to try the hotel restaurant and arranged a time to meet.

I love prawns and shellfish, so when I saw 'seafood and meat' on the menu I jumped straight in. 'That'll do for me,' I said. The other three just went for the meat option.

The food was cooked at the table and we were all given large bibs to wear. The chef started by getting out the beef, slicing it in front of us and then searing it on a hot plate. It looked and smelt delicious. Then he produced this massive king prawn, maybe eight or nine inches long, on a skewer.

With a great flourish, he placed it on the hot plate and immediately it jumped two feet in the air. It was still alive! The girls just screamed and fled from the table. Then he started cooking the prawn and every time he picked it up to turn it, we could see it wriggling away. Well, I was feeling worse and worse – I couldn't see any way I'd be able to eat it.

He finished cooking it, peeled it and placed it on my plate. With the chef looking on, I had no choice but to take a bite. I'm glad I did – it was the most beautiful thing I've ever tasted. As the girls came back, they saw I was eating it and couldn't believe their eyes.

The following day, we met up with Jonathan Greaves, who runs a company called Travelcare, which does all the official Manchester United trips and some England trips. He was really suffering with a bad back and wanted to get a massage, so we asked the hotel to book us in somewhere nearby.

They called us a cab and Jonathan, me and the guy from Middlesbrough jumped in. We had no idea where we were going but we were taken on a bewildering trip through the backstreets of Niigata, past all these wooden houses with ornately carved statues above the doors.

We eventually drew up outside a very modern building and

climbed out of the cab, not really knowing what to expect. The taxi driver pointed at the steps and motioned us to go in so we walked up the steps and saw scores of pairs of shoes lined up neatly outside. We took ours off as well and went inside.

The place was full of families, people of all ages, right from very old grandparents to small toddlers. We paid 1000 yen and were given a bath towel and a face towel each. We sat and waited and then this Japanese guy came out and asked if we wanted a normal massage or the hot oils. Me and my Middlesbrough pal opted for the normal massage, while Jonathan decided on the hot oils.

The three of us were taken into a small side room and told to lie face down on a table in the middle. As we got on to the tables, a screen was pulled aside and this tiny, elderly Japanese woman in an apron appeared. We could see another massage table behind her as she called Jonathan over and drew the screen back across.

Meanwhile, another woman and a bloke had come in to give the two of us a massage – and what a massage it was. The woman did mine and it was incredible. I lay there and she must have moved my legs into every possible position, twisted my arms round, and cracked all my knuckles. Then she turned me over and went to work on my neck, shoulders, torso – it was a proper going-over and took about 45 minutes.

Throughout, all we could hear from behind the screen was screams and shouts of pain. A couple of minutes after we'd finished, the old lady threw back the screen again. There was Jonathan, hair all over the place, looking like he'd been to hell and back.

'All right, mate?' I asked innocently.

'All right? All right? No I am bloody well not all right. I'm never having that again.'

'What happened? Sounded like you were enjoying it!'

'As soon as the screen came across, she got me to strip stark naked. Then she put a towel over my backside and got to work. First, she covered me in oil, then she got up, knelt on my back and massaged me all over. Then she turned me over and started on my front, massaging my legs and thighs. Then, all of a sudden, I started to get a bit of movement, you know, between my legs. She took one look and just said: "No, no, no" and waved her finger at me. I have never been so embarrassed in all my life.'

Of course, me and the lad from Middlesbrough were killing ourselves laughing but Jonathan didn't see the funny side until a lot later. After the massage, we went upstairs into a spa room with four different baths. We had to wash with soap first in a cubicle and then climb into the baths in order. The first one was about the same temperature as a hot bath, the second was a super-powerful Jacuzzi, the third was super-heated and the fourth was ice cold.

Once we'd been through that lot we wrapped our towels round us and were shown up on to the roof, where there were loads of Japanese people sunbathing. We were led to a sauna and told to strip off again but as soon as we walked in all the Japanese got up and left. Then we went to a steam room and from there into the pool for a final swim.

It was quite an experience, so good in fact we decided to do it again the next day – but that was when we paid the price for thinking we knew it all.

We marched through the front door and had our massage. Then we went upstairs again and straight through the first door on the right, just as we'd done the day before. But this time we were met by a crowd of naked Japanese women – I don't know who was more embarrassed, them or us, but we quickly shot out and went the other way.

We went to the Denmark game and saw England win 3–0, with first-half goals from Rio Ferdinand, Michael Owen and Emile Heskey, to put us in the quarter-final against Brazil in Shizuoka. So we headed back to Tokyo in a group which included Teddy Sheringham's mum and dad and Gareth Southgate's parents.

That was when I had one of the most frightening experiences of my life. We were sitting in the foyer of our hotel when suddenly I felt someone trying to pull the chair from under me. I grabbed on to the seat and looked round, just as the barmaid yelled: 'Earthquake! Earthquake!'

We were all terrified as the staff ran around opening doors and windows, desperately following the advice to lessen the impact of a big quake. But we could feel the building juddering, as though an express train was thundering past.

As quickly as it started, so it stopped. Everyone looked around nervously, as if expecting another impact. We later found out the centre of the earthquake had been 200 miles away – but even at that distance it was still a very scary experience.

In the build-up to the Brazil game, an old friend of mine, Barry Nevill, said he was going to the airport to meet Nicky Butt's mum and dad and wondered if I'd like to join him.

They were flying in for the game and, as I've known them since David joined United, I thought I'd go for the ride and I'm so glad I did because it was one of the funniest days of the whole World Cup.

As we arrived at Tokyo Airport, we saw Nicky Butt's mum Sue, and his brother Simon, coming through customs killing herself laughing. There was no sign of his dad, Terry.

Now Nicky's mum is a blunt Northerner and as she got to us, she blurted out, 'Can you believe it? They've only gone and arrested Terry!'

'Why, what's he done?'

'I've no idea. But they aren't letting him into the country.'

We turned her round and went back to the area where Terry was being questioned. He was in a small room off the main hall but we could hear every word he said, especially as Terry was getting more and more agitated.

'I haven't done a bloody thing. I'm telling you, I've done nothing wrong throughout my life.'

When his wife heard that, she just burst out laughing again: 'Can you hear what he's saying? What a liar.'

We were there for ages and all the time we could hear Terry pleading his innocence. In the end, Barry went up to the police desk and explained how embarrassing it would be if it came out that the Japanese had stopped an England player's family getting into the country.

He told them who I was as well and this policeman's eyes widened. Over and over again, he just kept saying, 'Be … ck … ham … Be … ck … ham … Be … ck … ham'. Then he went away and told a woman officer, who came out and, in halting English, asked: 'You Beckham father?' Of course, I told her I was but she still wanted to see my ID before she'd believe me. Eventually they let Terry in, much to everyone's amusement.

It turned out the name Terry Butt was on a police wanted list – apparently someone of that name was a known football hooligan who had to be stopped and turned away at the border if he tried to get into the country.

Terry was so relieved to be finally in the country but he nearly missed the Brazil match. He was in his seat and had stood up for a smoke, when suddenly about four stewards appeared from nowhere to surround him. We were watching from a few seats away and he looked terrified.

We, of course, were killing ourselves laughing. Terry hadn't known that you weren't allowed to smoke in Japanese grounds and you can be thrown out if you do. Luckily, they let him off.

There was a fantastic atmosphere inside the ground for what was probably the most eagerly anticipated game of the tournament. Every England fan believed we had a chance of beating the Brazilians and we went into the game feeling confident but nervous.

That confidence looked completely justified when Michael Owen put England ahead with a wonderful 23rd-minute goal, chipping the ball over the Brazilian keeper after a great through-ball from Heskey. It was thrilling to watch this England performance – we were more than holding our own against a team widely regarded as the best in the world.

But as quickly as our confidence had been born, so it was dashed away by the brilliance of the Brazilians. Deep into added time at the end of the first half, Ronaldinho ran at the English defence, who all backed off, before putting Rivaldo through to fire a left-foot shot past Seaman.

Worse was to come. Just five minutes after the break, Brazil were awarded a free-kick near the right-hand touchline, nearly two-thirds of the way back to the halfway line. All their forwards lined up to charge in on the inevitable cross as Ronaldinho got ready to take it.

But instead of crossing, his free-kick looped high towards the goal and went in past a stunned David Seaman. I'll never know if he meant it or not – I'm not sure he ever will, but it didn't matter – the Brazilians were ahead.

There was still more frustration to come for the England fans because Ronaldinho was sent off with more than half an hour to go after a reckless challenge on Danny Mills. The England fans all roared with delight as the referee produced the red card – with Brazil down to ten men we had a real chance of at least taking the game into extra time.

But that last half hour was desperately disappointing because England just couldn't find a way to break down the Brazilians. I heard several comments around me in the stadium having a go at Eriksson for not changing tactics, or making better substitutions and I think there must be a bit of a question mark over him about that.

David was very upset when Sandra and I finally got to see him afterwards. England were out of the tournament and he was heading home empty-handed again. He was in tears as we hugged him. It wasn't quite as bad as Argentina in 1998 but he knew we should have won the game, so that made it a very difficult defeat to take. I told him he'd done everything right. I think he took it particularly badly because he was the captain and felt a responsibility to his team-mates and to the country.

We flew back home with all the players on the England plane, as did many of the parents. I remember Nev was there, as were Michael Owen's mum and dad. I went around getting everybody's autograph, as I always did after big matches or big tournaments.

I took a ball round for everyone to sign, as well as a programme and a huge flag. I've still got them all and they are fantastic mementoes. I'm sure David will end up with them one day. I suppose I'm still a fan at heart and I still get a bit starstruck, even though my son is probably the biggest football star in the world. It is still a thrill for me to mix with these brilliant players.

We got back in the early hours of the morning to be met by Victoria, who was pregnant with Romeo, and Brooklyn. That made it a very special homecoming for us and for David.

He could look back on a season which had promised so much but had never quite delivered. The one consolation was that at least his new contract had been signed at United.

After the problems he'd had with Ferguson over his lifestyle and the negotiations, I was so relieved that his future was settled. I was more certain than I'd ever been that he would end his career at Old Trafford.

FROM
MANCHESTER
TO MADRID
2002-2005

'The game is now so huge and the level of expectation so high, that the players are under intense pressure to perform in every game. They say you're only as good as your last game, and that is truer today than it has ever been.'

David came straight out of the World Cup and into the frenetic pace of a new Premiership season. He has since admitted he wasn't really at the races at the beginning of that 2002–03 season – he felt tired and in need of a good, long break.

I don't think anyone can really understand the pressures players like him operate under. Everyone always thinks it must be great to earn your living as a professional footballer and, in many ways, it is. But the game is now so huge and the level of expectation so high, that the players are under intense pressure to perform in every game. They say you're only as good as your last game, and that is truer today than it has ever been.

David was jaded, both mentally and physically, in August 2002 and it hurt to see him like that. I could tell from those early-season performances that something was missing. As England captain, I think he had tried to shoulder a lot of the responsibility for the disappointment of the World Cup and that took its toll.

The attitude of Ferguson did not help, nor did a threatened kidnap attempt on Victoria, Brooklyn and the newly born Romeo, their second son. Thankfully, the police foiled that but it meant the security around them had to be raised to even more intense levels – another added pressure.

David certainly had a few problems with the Old Trafford boss in the first half of the season and it broke my heart to see their relationship fall apart.

The first hint of trouble came after David broke a rib in a Worthington Cup game against Leicester in November. In all honesty, neither David nor I could understand why he had even been picked for the game, even though he scored a penalty in United's 2–0 win.

United always rested their top players for the League Cup, but Fergie seemed to be making a point of playing David. It was as if he were trying to take him down a peg or two and prove a point about who was the biggest personality at Old Trafford.

Once David had got the injury, Fergie agreed he could go on a family holiday to Barbados but David delayed flying out so he could attend a reception at Buckingham Palace, hosted by the Queen, for England's World Cup squad. A broken rib takes four weeks to heal and there's not much you can do to speed that up.

When David eventually got back to Old Trafford, he was given the cold shoulder by Fergie – ignored in training and not involved in conversations. It took him a couple of weeks to have it out with Fergie and then it all tumbled out – Fergie reckoned he should have gone straight on holiday rather than attend the reception in order to get the healing process started more quickly.

I don't disagree with Fergie very often but I thought that was just petty. David was the captain of England and when the Queen invites you to Buckingham Palace, I don't think you've got much choice but to go. Fergie accused him of putting his own agenda ahead of United's, which David would never have done.

It seemed to me that certain players were allowed to get away with things that season, while others, notably David, were not. Fabien Barthez, for example, was given a week off to go on holiday around Christmas time, while David, the Nevilles and Nicky Butt were told to come in and train. That seemed so unfair – both the French and the English had played in the World Cup and the players were all equally tired.

David found that hard to take and he was hardly helped by the fact that Sandra and I were going through the final stages of our divorce.

David has spoken about how hard our splitting up was for him – it was tough for all our children. I know they were all pretty much grown up by the time we got divorced but it was still a heck of a shock for them. The last thing I wanted was for them to take sides. The problems lay between Sandra and me, not with any of them.

We'd been married for 33 years and had simply drifted apart. Just about the only thing we had in common was football.

I do not blame David in any way for our divorce but it was very difficult being the parents of someone so famous. All the hype, all the stress, all the attention – it wasn't a world we were used to and it was very tough. I don't think we were really prepared for it – although I'm not sure there's much you can do to prepare yourself. You just get swept up in it and bowled along. But it does wear you down.

I always told the children just to sit on the fence during the divorce. They all needed their mum and, hopefully, they all needed their dad. Whatever happens, they will always be our children.

David and his older sister, Lynne, knew of the situation long before Sandra and I finally got divorced at the end of 2002. Sandra and I had still gone to games together and we were both at the World Cup but things hadn't really been right for some while before then.

I must admit that I haven't really spoken to David about the divorce. He had his own problems at the time, so I took the decision that I would sort it out. It's something of a family trait with the Beckhams.

But we are not the only family to have gone through divorce and other families find a way through it. I'm sure we will but it's going to take time to settle down.

People have said David and I have drifted apart in recent years, first since he got married and then since the divorce. There's no doubt we see a lot less of each other than we used to but I think that's true of any father and son.

When your son is small, you see him every day but as he gets older that contact gets less and less. When he gets his own wife and family, they obviously take priority.

I don't think our new relationship is anything deliberate on either his or my part – it's just a fact of life. He knows I still love him and that I will always love him. And I'll always be here for him.

About halfway through what turned out to be David's final season at Old Trafford, we got a phone call at home from Ferguson. It came out of the blue but he wanted to meet with Sandra and me to talk about David. He asked if we would go and see him before the game on Saturday.

Of course, we were desperate to help, so we agreed straight away. When we arrived at Old Trafford we made our way to his office. It wasn't much fun listening to him talk through his concerns about David.

He said he wasn't happy with the way things were going and that he felt he could no longer speak to David. He was concerned at all the travelling he was doing, worried about his lifestyle and worried that he wasn't as focused on football in quite the same way as he had been in his younger days. Fergie asked if we would have a word with David and we promised we would.

We were deeply upset by that conversation. For the first time, I began to think that his future might lie away from Old Trafford.

I also know Fergie called Gary Neville and David in to see him together, to see if there was any way forward. David also met him on his own as well to discuss the future. Things were getting so bad that after the League game at West Ham in November 2002, Sandra collared Ferguson in a corridor at the ground and asked him what the real problem was. He just told her that 'everyone sucks up to David now'.

We did speak to David but he insisted everything was fine. He said he didn't think he was doing too much travelling and that everything was all right. He was quite angry that Fergie had even spoken to us. There were no problems, so there was nothing we could do to help. The conversation ended with my telling him to get his act together if he wanted to stay at Old Trafford.

Fergie continued to criticize David as the season wore on – sometimes justifiably, sometimes less so. He had a go at him after United drew 1–1 with Manchester City in February 2003 at Old Trafford, blaming him for giving away the ball too often.

Just six days after that game, came the infamous flying boot incident, which made headlines all around the world and put my son on all the front pages again.

United lost 2–0 to arch-rivals Arsenal and a furious Fergie laid into David after the final whistle. He blamed him for the second goal, saying he should have tackled back, and condemned his contribution to the whole match. As David tried to defend himself, Fergie angrily swung his foot at a boot which was lying on the floor.

I think it was destiny that it hit David in the face. Even if he'd been in another room, somehow that boot would have hit him.

In the heat of the moment, things like that happen. I don't think there was any malice or intent on Fergie's part – he was upset because we'd lost to Arsenal and he was trying to get his point across. We've all done things we regret when we're angry. He apologized straight away and that should have been the end of it.

I haven't discussed the incident in detail with David but I'm sure he accepted it as an accident. If you stop to think about just how hard it is to kick a boot into someone's face, I don't see how it could have been anything else.

There was a lot of rubbish talked about how David went out of his way to show off the cut the next day, going out with his hair pushed off his face with an Alice band. That was simply the way his hair was at the time – what was he supposed to do, hide in the house all day and not go out? It was typical of the way David is treated by the press.

I must admit to feeling more worried than ever that David might leave my beloved Manchester United. I didn't want to admit that possibility to myself but I think we all realized the writing was on the wall for David's United career when he was left out of the team for two vital games of the season.

The first was the Premiership trip to Arsenal on Wednesday, 16 April – a key game in the title race.

David had suffered a slight injury eight days before in the 3–1 Champions League defeat by Real Madrid in the Bernabeu. That meant he had sat out the following game against Newcastle, which United won 6–2, but was back in training two days before the Arsenal match.

He fully expected to play against Arsene Wenger's side and was devastated to be on the bench. That devastation was picked up by the press and made almost as big headlines as the game itself, which ended in a 2–2 draw to keep United three points clear of the Gunners at the top of the Premiership.

Worse was to come. With United needing a massive win over Real Madrid at Old Trafford to keep their Champions League dream alive, Ferguson had to start with his strongest team. And he left David on the bench.

David called me on the day of the game.

'Hi, mate,' I said. 'How are you doing?'

'Fine, Dad. But I'm on the bench tonight – I can't believe it.'

'What? I don't believe you … He wouldn't do that.'

'He has. He said he didn't think I'd ever had a good game against

Roberto Carlos and that he was making a few changes.'

'I can't believe it. But if you get on, take your chance to show him what you can do. You've got nothing to prove but just go on and do it.'

As everyone knows, Ferguson preferred a half-fit Sebastian Veron to David in midfield. It smacked of being a decision made for all the wrong reasons – to teach David a lesson, rather than to win the game. I can't believe Fergie would ever have put a personal argument above the interests of United but it was a very surprising decision.

Madrid were sensational that night, taking a 3–0 lead before the break; David came on during the second half – and he must have listened to what I'd said. He played superbly well, scoring two goals as United stormed to a heroic 4–3 victory. But it wasn't enough – Real had won the first leg 3–1, so that was good enough for an aggregate victory.

I suppose there had been some clues that Fergie was planning for life without David earlier in the season. He played Ole Gunnar Solskjaer in David's position on the right side of midfield in several key games, especially the win over Newcastle and the game at Arsenal. I think Fergie was seeing if Ole could handle that position although, as it turned out, the Norwegian got badly injured at the start of the following season so his plans were wrecked.

David did play the final three games of the season and I clung to the hope that he might somehow stay at Old Trafford. Indeed, I didn't really believe he was leaving until the final day of the season, when United were crowned Premiership champions for the fifth time since he had been in the team.

He scored in the 2–1 victory over Everton but somehow his celebrations, both for the goal and for winning the Premiership, were muted and half-hearted. He did not seem to fully share the joy of the others – something was missing. Even now, when I look at the video I can see him looking slightly distracted and not involved in the same way as his team-mates.

I've told him since that I knew he was leaving that day. He's said he can't understand that because he didn't even know then. Maybe it's a father's intuition but I knew he wouldn't be at Old Trafford the following season.

The week before, at the end of the final game of the season at Old Trafford David had taken Brooklyn out on the pitch. United had just beaten Charlton 4–1 and David had scored. He had a bit of a kickaround and looked around the stadium with a half-smile on his face. With the benefit of hindsight, I can see he was saying goodbye.

But, even at that late stage, I can't say I felt David would end up at Real Madrid. There had been some stories linking him with a move there at the time of the first leg of the Champions League tie but David had not mentioned it.

David and I didn't really discuss his problems with Fergie. I didn't want to make the situation worse by asking him about it and I knew he had Victoria and his agent, Tony Stephens, to confide in. I doubt he would have wanted to upset me by letting me know how bad things were. He preferred to keep all that to himself, which I can well understand.

I was always there for David and if he'd wanted my help, he knew he only had to ask. But he was a grown man and capable of making those decisions and dealing with those problems by himself.

I think we spoke just once more about it, right at the end of the season, when David told me he didn't think the club wanted him to stay. He told me they'd just offered him a new contract, which included a pay rise, even though he'd only signed his existing deal a year earlier. It was as if they were saying to him: sign or go, we're not bothered either way.

I couldn't bring myself to tell him how much that hurt me. I just told him it was down to what he and Victoria wanted and that they had a big decision to make.

Strangely, I had spoken to Victoria about the possibility of David leaving. I was over at their house one day and we were sitting round their kitchen table, discussing where he might go. I told her there was no way he could stay in England because United wouldn't sell him to any club that might be a rival for the Premiership – that ruled out Arsenal, Chelsea, Liverpool, Newcastle, so where else could he go? It had to be Europe.

She couldn't understand that at first but when I pointed out how United would feel if they sold David to Chelsea, for example, and he put three goals past them at Old Trafford, she grasped it.

As the season ended, it seemed clear his time was up, so it was no real surprise when I got a phone call from Tony Stephens telling me he was about to sign for Real Madrid. David was away on a sort of working holiday in America at the time but the £25 million transfer seemed to be sorted out very quickly.

I was pleased he had gone to such a massive club. I could still remember the great Real Madrid side of the 1950s, which won just about everything. They were the most glamorous team in Europe and only really have United for competition now. It certainly looks good on David's CV to have played for the two biggest clubs in the world.

I think United cashed in on him. I was particularly disappointed with Peter Kenyon, who was chief executive at United and now has the same job at Chelsea. I'd bumped into him when United played Spurs at White Hart Lane earlier in the season and asked him about David's future. He had assured me David would still be a United player the following season. I felt reassured by that but then he was sold. It was hard to take.

There was too much of a rift between him and Fergie for it to be healed. One of them had to go and it had to be David. But I think United and Fergie made a huge mistake by pushing David into a situation where he felt he had to leave. Fergie and David are both very stubborn people. Once they've made their minds up, it's all but impossible to get them to change.

David still respects Ferguson and he always will. He played such a huge part in making David the player he is today. But, just as importantly, David played a huge part in making Ferguson such a successful manager. I'm sure in a few years, both men will acknowledge the part the other one played in their lives.

It hurt like hell to think Ferguson wanted to get rid of my son. I'm still not sure whose fault it was or how the whole situation happened. As a United fan, I'm gutted because the team isn't as good without David. As a father, I know David wanted to finish his career at Old Trafford.

I was devastated when he left. My life and my enjoyment revolved around Manchester United and, especially, watching my son play for Manchester United. I know very few parents can ever experience that joy but when you've had it and it's suddenly taken away, it is bitterly disappointing.

I still have a host of mementoes and memories of his career and especially his time at Old Trafford. I've kept literally every medal, every award, every trophy, every kit, every picture from my son's footballing life. That includes all the stuff from his Ridgeway days and his junior days at Old Trafford – stuff he's probably forgotten he ever won.

Even today, I go through all the papers every day and cut out any article which mentions him. I've got literally thousands of clippings, some in albums and many others still waiting to be filed, which make up a complete record of his career.

I fully intend to let him have the whole lot when he moves back to England. It will form a magnificent collection to show to his sons.

I went to Old Trafford for the first game of the new season in August 2003 – their first season without my son – and watched Cristiano Ronaldo wearing David's shirt. We played Bolton and won 4–0. All my mates were up on their feet cheering but I just slumped in my seat and thought: 'What on earth am I doing here?' I wanted to get up and go. I felt completely out of place – I couldn't share in the thrill of the win because my son wasn't there.

I missed the next six games after that. I just couldn't bring myself to go – it was too painful. Without the support of my friends, especially Sam Chandrasingh, I'm not sure I'd have ever gone back.

Sam is originally from Sri Lanka but is a passionate United fan. He goes up from London for every game and he urged me to get back into it. He kept saying I was a United fan through and through and that I had to try and see it like that. I'm back to going every week now and, while it's certainly got easier, I know it can never be like it was.

I'm still a season-ticket holder but I don't get to see all the people I used to there – the tea lady, the people behind the bar, the receptionist – and I really miss all the banter that used to go on. I don't get to go behind the scenes as much as I used to and I don't go to the players' lounge now. I'm just an ordinary fan and that has taken a bit of getting used to.

I've also got Sam to thank for taking me to Euro 2004. We went over for the whole tournament and stayed on the Algarve. We were bussed up to all the games, which was a new experience for me because I'd only ever been part of an officially organized trip at previous tournaments.

We had a fantastic time and it was just what I needed after the emotion of David's departure from United. We fell in with a few lads who were staying near us and ended up having a fortnight to remember.

Unfortunately, I really stitched them up one night. I'd been to this great little restaurant on the beach front the night before and had really enjoyed their house speciality – giant prawns. They were fantastic so when about a dozen of us wanted to go out, I suggested we go back there.

The lads all piled in and I'd been talking up the prawns big-time. So as soon as the waiter arrived they all wanted the prawns and we ended up ordering 33 of them. I warned them they were massive but these lads were on a mission. They thought it was brilliant when the waiter came back to say they'd only got 26 giant prawns but they'd make up the difference with a few smaller ones.

When they arrived, the lads couldn't believe their eyes. These things were about 10 inches long and really thick. It was a huge amount of food and some of them had ordered a main course on top. But, to their credit, they waded their way through them and really enjoyed them.

What they didn't enjoy was the bill – £820! I think the prawns alone came to nearly £400.

We went to all the England games and watched most of the others in the bars in town. We were all shell-shocked by that first defeat to France. It seemed impossible to believe we were 1–0 ahead with 90 minutes gone, but still ended up losing 2–1. We'd reckoned without the brilliance of David's Real team-mate Zinedine Zidane.

Wayne Rooney is very much the new kid on the block and I don't know if he will go on to enjoy as wonderful a career as David – but he certainly announced his arrival on the major international stage in spectacular style against Switzerland in the next game. He scored two goals, with Steven Gerrard adding a third, to help England win 3–0.

And of course Rooney scored two more in the third group game as England dumped Croatia 4–2 to seal a quarter-final place against the tournament hosts, Portugal.

It seemed there were as many England fans as Portuguese in Lisbon's Estadio da Luz on that warm June evening. Yet again, the English supporters had turned out for a crucial game in a major championship with genuine hopes of success. And those hopes looked well-founded when Michael Owen put England ahead after just three minutes.

Sometimes you think your team may have scored too early in a game – 87 minutes is a very long time to hold on to a lead. That England managed to do just that for the next 81 minutes was something of a miracle but, with a mere six minutes to go, Portugal grabbed the equalizer through Helder Postiga.

That was enough to take the game into extra time. The first 15 minutes was played out cautiously, with both teams looking tense and nervy. The looming inevitability of a penalty shoot-out seemed to have got to the players. The fans were hardly daring to cheer, knowing that one mistake would spell disaster.

Then, five minutes into the second period of extra time, Portugal took the lead for the first time in the match thanks to Rui Costa. That was it – a black mood of despair gripped all the England fans around me. They didn't want to go home yet, but it looked like they'd have to.

They had reckoned without this England team and the driving passion which binds them together. It is something David has spoken about many times – the unique bond of friendship and team spirit which characterizes this squad. They needed every ounce of that to pull level – and that's exactly what they did through Frank Lampard with just five minutes to go.

The jubilation among the England fans was wonderful to see and I shared in it completely. We roared and cheered throughout those last five minutes – surely now the force was with England. Even if it went to penalties, we were convinced England would at last win a shoot-out in a major competition.

When the final whistle went, we stopped to draw breath. There is nothing quite like the tension of a penalty shoot-out. You know that just one kick separates joy from despair. There is no middle ground, no halfway house – you're either through to the next round or you're on the plane home.

No-one wants to be the man who misses the vital penalty, but it takes a special kind of man to take that risk. I can't say I was surprised when I saw David pick up the ball to take the first penalty of the shoot-out.

He walked calmly into the penalty area and spent an age stamping down the turf alongside the spot before placing the ball carefully on the ground. The stadium went silent as more than 65,000 fans held their breath in anticipation. David started his familiar run-up but as he planted his standing foot, the turf slipped away beneath him. As his kicking leg came through, he had no control and the ball ballooned away high into the crowd.

There was a moment of stunned silence before the Portuguese fans started cheering. The English fans' faces were contorted with anguish. I could not believe what had happened and my heart went out to him. He had been brave enough to take the first kick and he jogged back to the centre-circle with his head held high, desperate not to communicate his misery to his team-mates.

England ended up losing the shoot-out 6–5, with the Portuguese missing one before Darius Vassell missed a second one for us. It was another bitterly disappointing end to a tournament which had promised so much.

I didn't get to see David at all during the tournament because Victoria and Sandra were over with him and it was a bit awkward. But I've spoken to him since and I know he was very upset at the way it ended. It has only made him even more determined to succeed with England at the 2006 World Cup in Germany.

Of course, David going to Real Madrid has opened up a whole new life for me in going to watch them. It really is a fantastic club and a fantastic stadium. I usually watch from David's executive box but I don't have the same thrill at seeing Real win as I used to from United. The people in Spain are really warm and friendly, but there isn't that special closeness we had at Old Trafford. When all's said and done, I'm a United fan and I always will be.

It was certainly difficult for David at first. He told me he was a little in awe of all those world-class players, the so-called galacticos. He had always admired the likes of Ronaldo, Zinedine Zidane, Luis Figo, Roberto Carlos and Raul – now he was playing alongside them and was expected to be just as good.

I know he felt he had to prove himself to them but I always told him he had nothing to prove. The fact that Real Madrid were prepared to pay all that money for him was all the proof he needed that he was good enough to be there.

As I was telling him that, I remembered the time he was invited to play in Gordon Banks's testimonial game when he was just 20. He was in the dressing room with players like Gary Lineker and Gary McCallister and was totally gobsmacked by it. But he went out and played well that day, just as he has done for Real Madrid.

The only people he had to prove himself to were the fans. And he's certainly done that with both his skill and his work rate. I don't think the Spanish fans could believe just how hard he works for the team. Not all big-name players are prepared to do that, but David has always done it.

I've seen most of David's home games but his League debut will stick in my mind for ever. It was another part of the script which, if you were making it up, you would dismiss as too far-fetched. It was the first game of the season against Real Betis and David scored with his second touch of the game after just two minutes. Madrid went on to win 2–1. To call it a dream debut doesn't really do it justice – it was simply astonishing.

There have been some other great nights too, like the Real Madrid–Barcelona game back in April 2004 which Real won 4–2. Sandra was over there staying with David and Victoria, while I went with about a dozen friends to the game. I think I only got to see David for about five seconds during the whole trip but we had a wonderful weekend.

And David invited me over after his third son, Cruz, was born in February 2005 so we still have that special father–son closeness.

A lot of people have asked me about my grandsons' rather unusual names and, as you can tell from David's names, they wouldn't have been my first choice. But David and Victoria are always happy to make their own decisions and, when all is said and done, it's not the names that matter, it's the type of boys they are. And from everything I've seen of David as a father, I can honestly say I have no worries on that score.

I had a fantastic couple of days during that 2004-2005 season when I went to Milan to see United play in the Champions League and then drove from there to Turin to see Real play Juventus. The one down side was that both United and Real got knocked out but it was still a trip to remember.

David has struggled with the press in Spain. They are far worse than anything he experienced in England. He's told me that they are an absolute nightmare and if anything forces him back home the press intrusions will. He is being photographed almost every minute of every day, as are the children, which he finds especially difficult.

David wants to have as normal a life as possible. He wants to be able to take his boys to school or out for a hamburger without having to turn it into a military operation. But, unfortunately, his life isn't like that. He's been told not to take the boys to school because he'll be mobbed and that will frighten them. He cannot leave the house without security people around him – so everywhere he goes, he has to have minders.

And when he is out, he can draw a crowd of hundreds within seconds of getting out of the car. It makes even the simplest things in life hard for him – he can't just nip to the shops or go to the cinema or go for a meal. It all has to be planned.

He has some good people alongside him, especially Terry and Jenny Byrne, who take care of just about everything for him. Terry used to be a masseur with England and gave up a managerial job at Watford to go to Madrid with David. Terry and Jenny are both vital members of the team and make sure David is free to concentrate on his family and his football.

David has never spoken to me about the newspaper stories about his private life and I really don't think it's any of my business. He's a big boy now and that's between him and Victoria. I know what I read in the newspapers but I've never talked to him about it.

I respect him for the way he's conducted himself throughout his career. He's handled the good times well, accepting the adulation but never getting big-headed about it; and, perhaps more importantly, he's also handled the bad times well, with dignity and professionalism. I cannot speak highly enough of him. He sounds too good to be true but that's David to me. He is the perfect son and always has been.

I'm sure David is looking forward to the day when he can get some normality back in his life and I think that's why he's decided to start up his soccer academy. He has never wanted to go into management or coaching at a professional club – he hasn't got the right personality for it. He's not nasty, he's not vicious and he's not ruthless – and most great managers have a least one of those character traits.

David has always loved working with kids and I'm sure that is where he sees his long-term future. Now he's turned 30 he is looking to put something back into the game which has given him so much. He well remembers how important the Bobby Charlton schools were in his career and is very keen to give other kids the same opportunities he had.

The David Beckham Soccer Academy is based just next door to the Millennium Dome in Greenwich with two full-size pitches. And he's started doing soccer roadshows with Pepsi, which go all over the country. They've already been to Newcastle, Liverpool, Birmingham, Reading, Leeds, Manchester and London.

David's got his old United reserve team boss, Eric Harrison, on board to run the whole thing and pick the other coaches. It couldn't be in better hands. And when the kids see me and find out who I am they all want to come over and have a word. It's really great and I hope to get more involved in the future.

They've been brilliant and it's been great to see the look on the children's faces. As I stand on the side of the pitch watching them training, I cannot help but think back on my family's extraordinary journey. I look around at the eager parents and wonder if they will be next. And as I look at the children's joyful faces, I know one of them is destined to be the next David Beckham.

Acknowledgements

It is impossible to thank all the people who have helped to make David what he is today but they know who they are and I am deeply grateful to all of them.

Several deserve special mention. David's teachers, Mr Moore and John Bulloch who helped nurture the talent he was already showing. The coaches of David's district and county teams, Martin Heather, Pat Walker and Don Wiltshire who knew they were working with a special player and did everything they could to help him fulfil his potential. The special group of people who made up Ridgeway Rovers, especially Stuart Underwood and Steve Kirby, who were both great friends and great coaches.

At Manchester United, the late and much-missed Malcolm Fidgeon and his wife Joan, were incredibly supportive when David was starting at Old Trafford. Nobby Stiles, Jimmy Curran, Brian Kidd, Kathy Phipps and Annie and Tommy Kaye. Special thanks to Eric Harrison and of course Sir Alex Ferguson, both of whom believed in David and supported him every inch of the way.

Tony Stephens of course who helped David as he became more and more well known.

I must pay tribute to the people who helped bring this book about after many years of discussion. First, my great mate of 25 years, Barry Nevill, who has always believed in the project and encouraged me to do it. Also Tim Allan, whose help with writing the book has been fantastic, and everyone at Pan Macmillan, especially David North, Richard Milner, Natalie Jerome, Penny Price and Ingrid Connell.

Thanks too, to all the Beckham family – Sandra, Lynne and Joanne – who have all supported David on his journey.

Finally, thanks to David. It has been a pleasure to watch him from when he first kicked a ball to seeing him play in the World Cup Finals as captain of England.

I have been lucky. I have lived the dream of millions of parents who watch their children play, hoping that one day they just might captain England. My David did.